The More We
Find in Each Other . . .

D0029279

About the authors

Mavis and Merle Fossum have been married for thirty years and live in Minnesota, where they raised their two daughters. They enjoy spending time with their friends and engage in many outdoor activities, such as hiking, cross-country skiing, and camping. Mavis is a psychologist and a marriage and family therapist at the Family Therapy and Recovery Center in Minneapolis. Merle is a writer, social worker, and marriage and family therapist at the Family Therapy Institute in St. Paul.

The More We Find in Each Other . . .

meditations for couples

mavis fossum
merle fossum

▨ HAZELDEN

Hazelden Educational Materials
Center City, Minnesota 55012-0176

ISBN: 0-89486-793-8

Editor's note
Hazelden Educational Materials offers a variety of
information on chemical dependency and related
areas. Our publications do not necessarily represent Hazelden's programs, nor do they officially
speak for any Twelve Step organization.

CONTENTS

INTRODUCTION

We may find our most tangible encounter with the spiritual dimension in the mystery of a relationship. As two people who have unique histories and personalities in sharing our lives together, we create a third entity. Our relationship has no physical form, yet we know it exists. It is there in the space between us. It begins much as a seedling tree begins: undeveloped, thin, with no history, and casting little shade or influence. But in time it gathers force to exert great influence over our lives and the lives of others.

It grows into a complex combination of feelings and memories and disappointments and agreements, of the support we give to each other and the challenges we make to each other, of obstacles and frustrations that we have jointly faced, of our plans for the future, of the ways we make fun and play and the ways we satisfy each other.

The point is that while invisible, our relationship is certainly not hidden. We feel its power spreading through our lives as a growing tree casts its shade across a lawn. And it can either bless or plague our lives, sometimes doing both within a single hour. It is our unique creation. We influence its development, but it grows to influence us powerfully in return. The shape and pattern of our intimacy ultimately sweep us into places that surprise us, places that we did not want to go, and places that make us feel deeply grateful. When we are awake to what we are doing, we can join together as partners and shape our relationship into a force that blesses us, sustains us, and nourishes our individual lifelong development.

Even in the best relationships, intimacy is never a fixed piece of property that partners can own and hold like a special dish they bought at a store. It is a live organism that needs care and feeding. We nourish and sustain intimacy in the moments we take to reflect, to mark our experiences, and to notice each other. The simple ritual of a brief reading together can help us do that. As authors, we designed this book as a way for couples to consciously grow in intimacy.

Over the years of our own relationship, we developed the habit of taking a quiet moment together to read a brief thought, meditation, or quotation. We keep a book handy. Then just before dinner, or at bedtime, one of us reads aloud from it. Sometimes we talk for a moment about loosely connected thoughts and feelings that the reading brings forward. Some days when we can't read a passage together, we read alone. Quite naturally, our habit has grown into a simple ritual that we often do almost automatically. The wisdom of another person speaking from another time and place projects a light onto our particular experience that day. It soothes our tensions, heals us, reminds us of our blessings, and helps us find strength and direction. We hope this book will do that for you.

We are especially grateful to Judy Delaney, our editor, whose faith in this book helped bring it into the light of day and whose creative ideas helped shape its character.

. . . the more we find in each other.

We may have once dreamed of a mate with only attractive qualities. We probably wanted our mate to be good-looking, kind, strong, sexy, rich, fun, reliable, spiritual, athletic, gentle, gracious. Of course we did not want the opposites: ugly, hurtful, weak, awkward. Yet all human beings are complex and contain both attractive and unattractive traits. No one can ever fulfill our private, perfect dream. The more deeply we get to know our mate and the more intimate our relationship grows, the more we find in each other.

Sometimes our partner surprises us with a wonderful quality—a sense of humor, a helpful idea we had never known before. Other times words or actions deeply disappoint and hurt us. No relationship grows or deepens without that mixture. We do not shape and create our mate at our own pleasure or select him or her off the showroom floor as if we were buying a new car. True intimacy comes in knowing the many sides of each other, talking about them, having conflict, and making peace.

*Recall a conflict or disappointment
that you resolved in a
satisfying way.*

*We become bigger than
we could ever be alone.*

Our potential to give and receive love draws from a well of infinite depth, but only a small fraction of this potential ever gets developed. Love may grow and deepen within us throughout our lives, or it may lay undeveloped. Some people just grow colder and harder with each added year; others fill their spirit with love and warmth.

We might feel a natural impulse to hold ourselves back from the shaping wheel of intimacy. Yet we know that relationships are our great fortune. Relationships are schools for loving—and for being more human. In the struggles of listening, caressing, disagreeing, sometimes deflating each other's overinflated ego, apologizing for our wrongs, crying together, playing, forgiving, and believing in each other's talents, we become bigger persons than we could ever be alone.

*Make a list of people who have helped
you learn how to love.*

. . . when I finally gave up on my partner.

He believed that the love of his life, if he ever found the Right One, would fill all the gaps of his own personality. She dreamed that her perfect match would always respond gently, never willfully. After the honeymoon phase they naturally began to find imperfections and disappointments. Both wondered if they had chosen the Wrong One. But in a sense, there is no Right One for anyone. In another sense, there may be millions of Right Ones.

The closeness of a partnership will always reveal weaknesses and disappointments that were not obvious at first. No partner will match all the inventions of our own mind or so completely fit our needs that we have no remaining emptiness inside. One person said, "It felt like a terrible day when I finally gave up on my partner. But it became the first day of reality for me. Only after that did I discard the images I had invented for her and begin to get acquainted with who she really was."

For today, put all your ideas and desires for who your mate should become on the shelf and go only with who your mate is.

. . . the comfort we feel without our masks.

A mask is the image we use to cover an inner truth. And we need masks in some situations. Maybe we want to look competent when we apply for a job, or hide a weakness from others who would hurt us or take advantage of us. A police officer, for example, must give the impression of authority. Masks can also be fun, like when we get all dressed up in our fanciest clothes for a party. But a mask can restrain intimacy when we forget to take it off.

Real joy in intimacy comes with the comfort and liberation we feel without our masks. In taking them off we expose our weaknesses, admit our failures and successes. Our partnership grows by pushing the limits of what we are usually willing to risk. Then we can receive the rewards of acceptance, trust, and freedom.

Set aside your usual role for a time.
Maybe let yourself be humorous,
or tell a dream or a long-kept wish.

We live each moment
with more vivid awareness.

In our culture we can find ample ways to deny almost every unpleasant reality. Whatever we cannot control, whatever feels unhappy, we can avoid by watching television, shopping, or chasing some other external stimulus. Even the death that awaits us all—the ultimate reality and loss of control—is widely denied. But we become much stronger, more grown-up, and wiser when we let the bad news as well as the good into our daily lives.

If we remember that at some point our lives together will not continue, we live each moment with more vivid awareness. Playing as if life were just a game, we continue to compete with each other, withhold satisfaction from each other, and reserve an edge of power over each other. When we move beyond denial, life does not become grim or morbid, it becomes more worthy of love and celebration. When we see with our grown-up eyes that *this is it*, we do not hold back our expressions of love.

Find a way to express your love today.

. . . take some risk to express our love.

Some of us keep our strongest feelings to ourselves. We feel sad, frightened, or deeply loving and do not risk showing this to others. But as a couple, we get together to share our lives, not to guard against each other. And love is more than a private inner feeling. It is also an action. So we must go against comfortable habit and risk expressing our love. When we do, we show faith that our actions will multiply, that we will have even more love, more giving and receiving than we had before.

Love pushes us to show our feelings to the one we love. But even with our life partner, to say how we feel might seem risky. We want to hold back and keep control. Now we must overcome hesitation because stifled love diminishes. When we say in words, "I love you," when we say it with a touch or a look, when we do a thoughtful thing or listen fully for a moment to our partner, we grow in the healthy expression of love.

Express your love in words
or actions right now.

It was not a disagreement,
it was a misunderstanding.

He said, "Let's go to the movies when we're done with our work." She said, "That's a great idea!" But when the work that she had in mind was finished, he still had several tasks that remained undone. So they got into a dispute. It was not a disagreement, it was a misunderstanding.

Another day, she said she was frightened about an upcoming visit to her doctor. Actually, she felt overwhelmed with fear and was trying hard to keep herself under control. But on the outside, she looked controlled, so he thought she was only a little afraid. She felt hurt and neglected because he seemed insensitive to her great fear.

What one means and thinks on the inside will never be exactly what one shows in words and feelings on the outside. We naturally long to be understood. But in adult relationships we have to expect differences between what is meant and what is said. This has nothing to do with honesty or how much two people love each other. What seems obvious to one partner on the inside is not necessarily obvious to the other partner on the outside.

Recall a time when your words did not
convey your whole meaning.

We can put aside all judgments.

When lovers communicate sexually, they find bliss in their connection. By judging our sexual performance, some of us get anxious and lose track of our communication. This is like evaluating the paper and ink in a daily newspaper without reading the news. It is a game that distracts us from the pleasure and communication that we seek. Rating performance fits more with athletics than with sexual communication.

By letting go and letting God into our sexual lives, we can put aside all judgments of ourselves, making sexuality a spiritual part of a loving, honest relationship. Then sex may be just a soft touch on the neck, lying together, skin touching skin while the rest of the world is closed out, or it may be total bodily surrender to each other.

Tell your partner one way
you appreciate being touched
and one way you like to give touch.

. . . building our whole relationship . . .

Sex is often thought of as a barometer of other aspects of our relationship. But sex is not the foundation of our connection with each other. When sex is not good, it can mean that there are other ways we are missing each other. Are we taking time to nurture our relationship, or are we like ships that pass in the night? How often do we take time for just the two of us?

Adventure, play, and reflection make a more solid foundation for our sexual relationship. When we create time together for sharing our joys and our sorrows, time to play and just act silly with each other, we strengthen our foundation. When we put our energy into building our whole relationship, sex becomes more fun and more fulfilling.

Plan a time to relax and play together.

. . . showing who you
are behind your mask.

The intimacy of sex is like inviting someone into the most personal, most confidential place in your home. It is like playing your most treasured music to a friend. It is like taking the risk of showing someone a picture you drew, a poem you wrote, sharing a secret—showing who you are behind your mask. It is like having a friendship that is trusting enough to cast aside all inhibition. Sex is showing your true feelings for the joy of making a connection and trusting that you will be accepted. With no risk, trust, or acceptance, sex might still be a release but it is not always intimacy.

The intimacy of sex requires that we know and love ourselves. Otherwise, we will not dare to let someone else know and love us. Such intimacy does not happen overnight. It grows with time spent together, builds on misunderstanding and its resolution, thrives on feeling accepted and finding ways to accept the person we are with.

Tell your partner one intimate detail
you value about him or her.

*. . . openly expressing our affectionate
feelings . . .*

Men and women often have different needs and
find different meaning in their sexual experiences.
One partner might emphasize the emotional connection over the physical connection; the other
partner might emphasize the physical connection
over the emotional connection. How do we deal
with the difference? We start by accepting that we
both want connection. We recognize how our partner wants connection and we try to be understanding. We don't have to give up what we need for
ourselves. But if we insist that our partner change
to meet our needs, we will most surely become
unhappy, disappointed, or lonely.

Connection is what we both want. How can we
make it happen? Simply and openly expressing our
affectionate feelings at any time of the day builds
our union. We need to touch base with each other
often to affirm our relationship. When we do, our
sexual and emotional communication grows as an
important part of one whole, intimate, life-giving
experience.

*Tell your partner how you feel about your
sexual and emotional contact.*

*. . . we have some unfinished business
between us.*

When we respond to the small signals that something is amiss, we prevent bigger problems. When we feel fear in our relationship, it signals that we have some unfinished business between us. When we ask the questions we have been avoiding, we create new possibilities for resolution. Our fear is a signal that something does not feel safe. If we tell ourselves that our fear is illogical and discount it, or if we overreact by totally pulling out of the situation, we miss opportunities to change it.

What a relief we feel as we make sense out of our fear and begin to talk with each other. We let go of secrets between us and work toward mutual understanding. As we communicate, the knot in our stomachs loosens and light reappears in our relationship.

*Name the signals your body gives you
to indicate that something in your
relationship needs attention.*

. . . alone in the company of our partner.

To be alone in the wilderness is less painful than to feel alone in the company of our partner. When we shut down in silence because we feel wounded by our partner, we slam the door on healing. We may justify emotionally abandoning our partner by telling ourselves that we do not want to be hurt again, and we may be convinced that our partner is never going to change anyway. We each have our own style of "going away" and our own way of maintaining our loneliness.

When we feel the pain of separation from each other, we need to reach back and reopen communication. We can do that by telling our partner how we disappeared and asking her or him to join us in healing the wounds. When we talk about our feelings and we are understood, we make genuine contact and we are no longer alone!

*As a way to enhance your connection now,
tell your partner about a way that
you have disappeared.*

We wonder, How can I ever say this?

We need to be free to talk about anything in our intimate relationships. Some things are very hard to say—an old secret we have never told before, a feeling or an observation our partner does not want to hear, a mistake we made that calls for confession. We wonder, "How can I ever say this? How can I avoid hurting myself or my partner?"

Not all things need to be said at once. Readiness is the first part. We can get ourselves ready to speak. The second part is timing. When we are ready, we wait for a good moment to appear, a moment in which our message will fit. The third part is love. Honesty coupled with care and love is healing and strengthening. Some pain is necessary in a growing relationship, and we can tolerate it because it leads to more understanding and more peace of mind.

Think of one new thing you would like to tell your mate about your thoughts, feelings, or behavior.

*Grief may be a pathway
to our deepest connections.*

People often say, "I don't want to burden you with my troubles, you have enough to worry about." Yet sharing our troubles with our partner or close friends lightens our burden and restores our balance. Telling someone our experiences and how we feel about them helps us find and create the meaning that lurks behind them, even though they at first seem only crazy and random. Sharing with others pulls us out of isolation and brings our friends and mate into the circle of our lives.

We may be surprised to feel the knots in our stomachs loosen when we tell our stories and recount our worries or grief. Grief may make us feel more alone than anything. But it may also be a pathway for our deepest connection with each other. When we reach out and talk with our friends or mate, we break down the wall of isolation and build bridges that connect us.

*Tell your partner about any grief
you carry today.*

*. . . what we want
more deeply than winning.*

When our relationship is in conflict, we may think that our partner always has the last word. We think it would feel good, just once, to come out on top. If our relationship is like a poker game, the winner takes all. We scramble to be the winner at almost any cost. If our partner wins, we feel like the loser. If we score a point, then our partner feels like the loser. In the end, if either one has lost, what have we won? Certainly not serenity.

What do we really want in our relationships? Do we want to stay in the fight until we score the final knockout? No. We want companionship and connection. To get beyond the game, one partner must stand up and say what she or he wants more deeply than winning. When we stand in favor of communication, our relationship improves.

*Name what you really want
in your relationship.*

The adventure of connection
is to speak out . . .

The feeling of connection we yearn for with our partner comes when we speak what is on our mind. We have to stop guessing what each other feels and stop guarding against all offenses. A relationship with vitality is not so guarded that we constantly have to avoid rubbing each other the wrong way. We expect offenses and misunderstandings occasionally.

The greatest offense we can commit in an intimate relationship is dishonesty. Perhaps when we speak to our partner we will not express what we really mean on our first try. Or we will not realize how our partner feels about what we say until he or she tells us. In vibrant and living relationships people agree that they will keep talking when someone feels hurt, misunderstands, or disagrees. The adventure of connection is to speak our thoughts and feelings in their complete form, and then continue to talk until they become clear and understood.

Tell your mate something you have been guarding in your mind.

. . . we may surprise ourselves
by discovering a treasure.

Not all secrets are bad. Some secrets are more like unspoken, unacknowledged mysteries than sinister destructive forces. We may quietly know what it is like to be a man or a woman in an intimate relationship, but we may never have told anyone in words. We may have a sense of how our lives have changed as a result of our relationship, but we may never have stopped to fully express it, even to ourselves. A piece of music may touch a place within us that does not have words. Those secrets are valuable and worth guarding like a precious treasure.

When we try to find words for these secrets, we may surprise ourselves by discovering a treasure. They may give us a sense of power or join us with others who understand us. These treasured secrets are an adventure for a couple to reveal to each other. What is the most valuable lesson you have learned about intimacy since you first met? What would you reveal to your son or daughter about the ways to gain the greatest happiness in love? How would you choose to live the last day of your life?

Select a treasured
secret to tell your partner, and
then try to describe it to him or her.

Our silence can keep us isolated.

"Still waters run deep" may be true for lakes and rivers, but in intimate relationships it is not necessarily true. Our silence can keep us isolated from ourselves and from those we love. In order to grow together, we must let each other know how we think and feel. Sometimes just saying a thought or feeling helps us see beyond it.

If we keep our thoughts to ourselves, we may get so immersed in those still waters that we nearly drown in them. A problem kept to ourselves usually grows bigger and more consuming. When we talk about it we can work through it and move on to something else.

Choose one concern, small or large,
and express it to your partner.

. . . we first look to ourselves.

We may do something that we do not want our partner to know, perhaps something that puts us in a bad light. If we lie about it, what do we gain? Our secret may be safe, but we have put another brick in the wall that prevents us from having an open intimate relationship. Our white lie does not protect our relationship, it damages it. By chipping away at our self-respect, we also damage our relationship to ourselves. Before long we become suspicious of others, believing that they also are not as they say, or that they are manipulating us.

By this process we project the infection in our soul onto our partner. If we believe he or she is manipulating us, perhaps we need to face our own manipulation. Our partner may have defects, but to help our relationship grow, we first look to the only one we can change, and that is ourselves.

Think about your honesty with your partner.
Can you improve your relationship by
clearing up a misleading message
you have given?

. . . armed to deal with whatever comes.

One couple never told each other anything negative if they could avoid it. They always protected each other from bad news. Their neighbors, however, were not that careful about what they said. They had a positive attitude but they believed that reality was not to be shaped or measured in their words, so they just laid it on the line with each other. The first couple seemed more sedate and calm while their neighbors seemed more in turmoil. But over time the first couple's protective attitude worked like a wedge that drove quiet distance between them as more and more unresolved issues were ignored or sugar-coated. The second couple always clearly knew what was going on. They did not have to wonder what the truth was behind each other's words, and they dealt with issues as they arose. Time brought them more deeply into the lively embrace of their trusting relationship.

Bad news is part of life, just as good news is. When we engage life we do not shy away from problems; we do our loved ones the favor of speaking the truth. Then our relationships are armed to deal with whatever comes.

Describe how you deal with good news
and bad news in your relationship.

. . . stepping stones for moving on.

Of course we have some fears. Every human being on earth has fears, whether she or he lives in a quiet solitary hut along a footpath in the mountains, in an apartment along a noisy city street, or in a three-bedroom rambler in the suburbs. Perhaps we worry about the dangers or the hard times we will face in the future. Or we worry about accidents, crime, bills, health, war, the environment, and our children. Once we start, we can make a long list of fears. Actually writing down that list or drawing pictures of our fears helps us confront them.

Words and pictures symbolize our inner experience—they help us name and describe our fears so we can face them and regain our power. If we avoid expressing our fears, they can control us. Once faced, our fears are not blocks but stepping stones for moving on. Then we can remind ourselves again that we live only a day at a time. We can face what we must this day and leave tomorrow's problems for tomorrow.

Express one of your greatest
fears to your partner.

Sometimes support means
bringing the bad news.

A couple's relationship is a mutual support agreement. The relationship that works is the one that supports the best in both people. That means encouraging our partner to take risks when he or she wants to improve or try something new. It means noticing each other's strengths and saying what we appreciate. And sometimes support means bringing the bad news, not agreeing to go along with harmful actions, speaking an unappealing truth that no one but a loving partner would speak.

At times, we may fall silent in our relationship. Something within wants to hold back from saying what we appreciate, how we feel, or what we believe. It is easier for some people to tell a third person what they like about their mate than it is to say it directly to him or her. Do we hold back our applause and support? We need to ask ourselves, "Is that how I want to be? Do my actions lead me where I want to go? Do they fit my values?" Spirituality grows from raising our consciousness.

Tell your partner some things
you like about her or him.

*Respect grows out of time
spent together.*

The simple word *respect* carries profound meaning for an intimate relationship. One might be suddenly attracted to a person, have a passionate love affair with that person, and enjoy the companionship a great deal. Yet respect grows out of time spent together, learning to know someone's finest qualities in daily routine and under stress, and bringing one's own self-esteem to the relationship. Respect is the keystone of a durable love.

Respect is a love message. It is listening quietly to what someone wants to tell us and expressing our wishes and opinions openly. It is making eye contact, touching gently, saying hello when someone arrives and good-bye when he or she leaves, intruding on another's privacy only with permission, and letting a partner make his or her own mistakes.

*Tell your partner the one thing you respect
most about her or him.*

. . . support to respond in new ways.

There are times when our partner does something that is so infuriating that we want to strike out and make him or her hurt. We may want to yell or curse or become physically abusive. Other tactics are more subtle, but every bit as hurtful. We may give our partner the silent treatment or belittle him or her around friends or family. Or we may portray ourselves as helpless victims to make others angry at our partner. When we resort to these methods to attain "justice," we maintain the abusive system we hate.

Talking to a trusted friend, a therapist, or our Higher Power can give us support to respond in new ways. With guidance we learn to resolve conflicts without maintaining the war. It is easy to find reasons to support a stubborn position, but the real work of our relationship is to listen and to understand where the other person is really coming from. Then, after understanding, forgiving ourselves and our partner comes easily.

What have you learned about dealing with moments when you want to strike out at your partner?

. . . leave our weapons at the door.

Sometimes we pull back from emotional contact with our partner when we have conflicts that remain unresolved. We put up a fence between us rather than engage in working things out. Perhaps we do it as a power game to see who will give in, start talking, or apologize first. We may even silently think this is a test of love. "If she loves me she will come to me." When people play this game, they do not realize how much they pay.

Because we are partners, our communication follows different rules than many other relationships we have. We both agree to leave our most hurtful weapons at the door and never use them against each other. We agree that we can show our weaknesses to each other, and then we agree not to take advantage of them. This allows us to take down the barriers we build against each other and not become imprisoned behind them. Then the relationship frees us and makes us stronger than we could be alone.

Name an emotional barrier
you feel trapped behind.

*. . . resolve things
without the destructiveness.*

A lovers' quarrel is a fight that is made more intense by the passion and vulnerability we feel in our closeness. Were it not for the intimacy and passion between us, our feelings would not be so sensitive; we would be able to settle our differences with less heat and more light on the subject. The passion of a fight between lovers sometimes gets hotter, more hurtful, or more destructive precisely because we care so much about each other and because we feel so vulnerable to each other.

In the midst of a fight, just remembering that *this is a lovers' quarrel* can help us put it into perspective. We are not fighting like this because we hate each other. We are fighting like this because we love each other. Perhaps we feel afraid. We can then cool down so that we resolve things without the destructiveness.

Name a time you had a lovers' quarrel.

. . . a new level of personal dignity.

Over time we are each treated to the full range of what the other has to dish out. We may put out our worst at times of great stress. Maybe we feel sick, face unemployment, or feel personally attacked in an argument. These events seem like a threat to our survival or our dignity and strain our ability to cope. When we feel our self-respect is under attack, we are most likely to react with an attack on our partner's dignity.

As we become more conscious in our relationship, we can tune in more quickly to our feelings. When we feel our dignity or survival is threatened, do we say or do hurtful and vicious things to our partner? Perhaps when something feels out of control we can stop to notice if we feel our dignity or survival is at stake. Then we can choose not to react with our first impulse but to say how we feel. When we do that, we achieve a higher level of personal dignity.

*Name the stress that brings you
to your lowest level of maturity.*

Anger can be
constructive and creative.

Anger is a powerful emotion. It can release the energy we need to stand up for what is right and defend our survival. Anger expressed in respectful yet angry ways can be constructive and creative. Many of us have been intimidated by others who have used their anger in abusive ways, or we have been frightened by our own loss of control when angry. We did not learn to separate anger from abuse.

Emotions are neither good nor bad, but couples develop good and bad patterns for handling anger in their relationship. Some couples always blame each other when frustrated; others have one partner who always blames and the other who always accepts the blame. Some belittle and attack each other's character; others never let any expression of anger rise to the surface because of fear. Still others get hooked on anger and only feel alive when they are going at it. Growing in intimacy requires that we not bottle up our true feelings or express them in attacking or belittling ways, but that we express them openly and respectfully.

Think of a time you or your partner
expressed anger openly and constructively.

Talking comforts us
and dispels tension.

Our automatic reactions come from our human nature and from memories of past difficulties. Under stress we naturally tense our muscles and minds to prepare for flight or fight. Conscious choices can take us beyond these automatic fear *reactions* and help us use more creative *responses*. We can learn to stay serene when facing our fears rather than react automatically.

We can talk about our feelings with each other. Just talking comforts us and dispels tension. We can also pray and meditate, not to control what we have no power to change, but to accept the ultimate care and wisdom of a Power greater than ourselves. We can keep returning to the simple wisdom of living just one day and one moment at a time. We do not have to deal with today's troubles plus all the troubles we foresee. With practice we can determine to *respond* with our integrity and not be victims of our automatic *reactions*.

Make a list of your worries
and then consciously turn them over
to the care of your Higher Power.

. . . we can listen to our inner truth.

To make distinctions between what is truly important and what is trivial requires many years of experience. It requires the courage to stand aside from popular beliefs or from immediate pressures so that we can listen to our inner truth. We arrive there only after some pain and perhaps after pursuing a few exciting and tempting dead ends. Many of us know the feeling of crushing pain or disappointment after events that did not turn out as we had planned. We may have these experiences together, and together we learn wisdom.

After learning from life experiences we become wiser, and we have a stronger foundation on which to stand. We are like the man who was afraid of looking bad in front of his friends until he had a heart attack and almost died. "After facing death and surviving," he said, "appearances aren't important at all. What kind of person I am is far more important than how I look."

*Tell your mate one thing
that is more important to you
than appearances.*

. . . a genuine apology when it is deserved . . .

Some of us easily slip into a pattern of saying "I'm sorry" every time our mate is offended or unhappy with our actions. We want to please, or we hate conflict, so we choose the appearance of peace and its good feelings rather than trying to truly resolve and repair problems. Genuine repair starts with regret and follows up with efforts to change our behavior or attitude. If we just give empty apologies and do not back up our words with actions, we put ourselves down and drain the trust from our relationship.

A genuine apology is personal, clear, and specific. It suggests a change in future behavior. The personal part says I am sorry that I hurt *you*; the clear and specific parts name exactly what action we regret; and then we say how we will make repair. If we say, "I'm sorry you feel bad," we are expressing sympathy, but we are not apologizing for our behavior, because there is no specific action that we regret. Giving our partner a genuine apology when it is deserved and backing it up with action is the best way to inspire respect and trust.

Tell your partner a change
you are making or striving to make
that comes out of an apology.

We get angry because we care.

Strong feelings keep us involved with each other. We may not give it a second thought when someone we barely know makes an angry remark. But if our partner's voice gets a certain tone, or if just one eyebrow is raised, our blood pressure jumps. Is it written in our mind that the perfect relationship should be all positive and easy? Does anger make us wonder if this is the right relationship? Lifelong partnerships are vastly deeper than the "wonderful" relationships portrayed in some romantic songs.

We get angry because we care. We express our feelings, including the negative ones, and in doing so we affirm our connection. We could say, "I'm angry and I'm telling you about it so that we can work it out." The alternative—to feel angry and swallow it—undermines our connection and creates distance. Learning how to give and take strong feelings and then resolve them is a major task in a long-term partnership.

Remember a time when a disagreement deepened your connection.

. . . expand our focus . . .

Sometimes conflict persists and builds in our intimate relationships not because we want to inflict harm, but because we are committed more to our own viewpoint than to resolving the fight. If we are set on the idea that our partner is wrong, dishonest, controlling, or making us feel crazy, then that is all we will see.

Change requires that we stop to look at our own part in a conflict and make honest efforts to understand our partner's point of view. Sometimes our determination to win is maintaining the conflict. If we will surrender our determination, we can begin to listen to our partner's point of view. If we stay focused exclusively on our own outlook, we cannot understand how our partner sees things. To truly listen we do not have to give up our opinion; we only have to expand our focus to include our partner's viewpoint. Then we open the door to true intimacy.

Tell your partner something you learned about him or her in a recent conflict.

SEPARATENESS

*Intimacy is the bridge
between our differences . . .*

We need balance in all things. The excitement and joy of attraction can draw us into a relationship so tightly that we neglect our individual development. That can stifle our individuality for the sake of our connection. Without separateness we cannot have true intimacy. Intimacy is the bridge between our differences, the meeting of our separateness, not the merging or obliteration of differences. The opposite is equally true: that excessively pursuing separate wills and individual goals without giving generously to each other and to joint goals leaves only distance—and no bridge.

Sometimes the happiness of our partner feeds the happiness of our relationship and ourselves. When our partner goes off without us to pursue his or her favorite pastime for an afternoon or a weekend, it nourishes our whole system of intimacy when it is balanced with togetherness. Likewise, a hearty disagreement between us can be a healthy meeting of differences when we continue with it through to resolution.

*Name your separate interests that give
vitality to the spirit in your house.*

*It is a betrayal of the relationship
to sacrifice self-care.*

It is truly loving to take care of ourselves. When a person is so self-sacrificing that all self-care is neglected, it is a betrayal of the relationship. If we regularly feel too tired, too busy, too preoccupied, or too ill to enjoy the rewards of friendship and emotional contact with our partner, then we are dropping our part of the bargain.

We have an obligation to notice our own needs, to look after ourselves like a treasured friend, and to make room for our needs with others. That does not mean "me first," but it means there is room for everyone. If we constantly defer to others' needs, we may be present only in body, not in spirit. True intimacy cannot occur when one person is an empty shell. When we speak up to each other, our needs will naturally conflict at times. That is a sign of vitality, so we search for solutions that make room for both persons' needs. A basic rule for intimate relationships is: We will pay each other the honor of saying what we want and need, and then talk about it to make room for our differences.

*Name a personal need
and how you are taking care of it.*

We can go to a sanctuary within.

Constantly thinking about and trying to control our partner can create an invisible shield that stands between us, stifling our intimacy. The problem is that in our preoccupation we lose contact with our own inner stillness. We sacrifice our needs in order to control our mate. When we think we can control anyone but ourselves we live in a delusion. Our best intentions with control lead only to more stress.

When we have made peace with ourselves, we can go to a sanctuary within. Whenever relations with others are in turmoil, we can retreat to that place and be calm, knowing that we can only control ourselves. Then, with each other, we stand on a solid foundation of inner stillness.

Name a situation where you need the wisdom to distinguish between what you can change and what you can only accept.

. . . claim authority over ourselves.

Sometimes seeing ourselves through someone else's eyes can be a virtue. Indeed we need that ability in order to empathize and connect with others. Yet taking that virtue to its extreme, we see our life only as someone else sees it, evaluate our actions only by others' standards, and never claim authority over ourselves. Seeing our life only through someone else's eyes leaves a hole in the center of our own life. We may be afraid to grasp our right to see our life through our own eyes. Others will not always understand; we will make mistakes that we must repair; someone might get angry at us. But we have a right to mistakes too.

When we develop a sense of our self, a feeling of our strength, and see life through our own eyes, we become full partners in our relationship.

Describe an incident or a way in which you viewed your life through someone else's eyes.

. . . risk creating our own life path.

Sometimes it seems easier to lean on our mate for all decisions and all direction. Then we do not have to risk creating our own life path. Some people think they can avoid that risk by striking a bargain with their mate. They so fully immerse themselves in their mate's identity that they never have to face their own. Some couples unconsciously agree that one partner will do all the thinking and the other will have all the feelings. The result of their bargain blunts the spirit of both people, because neither grasps the challenge to see life through her or his own eyes. When both of us know how it feels to walk in the other's shoes but still see our life through our own eyes, we find the greatest personal empowerment and spiritual freedom.

Think of a time when
your relationship was stronger
because you took the risk to be different.

. . . returning to our inner vision . . .

We may feel far removed from our childhood family experiences. We may even want to set ourselves apart from the family patterns we grew up with. But as surely as we bring our fondest hopes into our intimate love relationships, we will also face disappointment and unhappiness. We will see that sometimes we do not hold up our end of the relationship. Perhaps we will say to ourselves, "If only my partner were different, I would be happier," placing blame for our discomfort outside of us. The challenge is to say, "My unhappiness is within me. If I lived alone a hundred miles away from here, sometimes unhappiness would still rise up from within me."

Let's not say there are no real relationship problems that create unhappiness. But our task is to keep returning to our inner vision and distinguish between what is our work as individuals and what is our relationship work.

Describe the time when you
first saw a vision for what your
relationship could be.

Moving into wise
and spiritual adulthood . . .

At our worst we may be alert to what we want from our partner but blind to what our own role requires. No doubt we can always find accurate criticisms of our mate. In all lasting relationships we will find the weaknesses and the unattractive sides of even the finest people. Finding them in our partner means little when our hope is for a good and successful partnership.

We each walk an individual path. No one else can take our footsteps. No one but us can live our unique life stories. That is the hard truth that adults have to face and children do not. The joys and pleasures of adult intimacy grow when we know our separateness. We will always yearn for a past childhood or for an unfulfilled dream enveloped in the generous care of loving parents with no stress and no demands. But as adults we live in an insecure world, and no partner can ever create that security for us. We move into wise and spiritual adulthood when we expect imperfection around us and develop a core of inner peace.

Describe a dream of peace and security
that you keep in your memory
or in your imagination.

We all have some inconsistencies.

We naturally draw an invisible line that separates what we say and do around casual friends from what we say and do with intimate partners and family. Our feelings of friendliness and openness are different on each side of the line, and we usually feel more relaxed in intimate surroundings than we feel in public places. This line that quietly separates public situations from private ones helps us define who we are and what our relationships are like.

We can learn something about our spiritual vitality by asking how our private actions and attitudes match our public ones. They are naturally different, but are they compatible? Do we live out the appearance and attitudes in private that we convey publicly? Some people always show an optimistic and generous face in public but are bitter, resentful, and domineering in private. Some show rigid morality to others but in private they cut corners morally. We all have some inconsistencies. Honesty about them shows us our spiritual incompleteness, and we grow when we face them.

In what ways are your public
and private actions consistent?
In what ways are they inconsistent?

. . . no one could fill all of our needs . . .

Sometimes we take comfort in thinking that our unhappiness is caused by our mate. If our needs are not met, if we feel a deep emptiness or desire that goes unsatisfied, if we feel angry, we blame our mate. We say, "If only you were different, I would be happy!" We are uncomfortable admitting that our biggest problem might be ourselves. Sometimes no one could fill all of our needs—no matter what. Perhaps, in our overdependence, we become dissatisfied. We would feel better if we would stop indulging in delusions of blame.

Awareness of the truth may make us feel uncomfortable, but then it empowers us. When we stop searching the kitchen for keys that we dropped in the hall, we stand a better chance of finding them. And when we stop looking outside ourselves for the cause of our internal frustrations, we may find what we need.

Tell your partner a desire you have. Then add in your own words that you know your feelings about it are your own responsibility.

Sometimes help doesn't help.

When we see loved ones do things that hurt themselves, we hurt too. When they act self-defeating or are addicted or when we see their pain and the trouble they cause themselves and others, we might gladly turn ourselves inside out for them if it would help. But it would not.

Sometimes help doesn't help; it gets in the way. A truly respectful love stands by in loving contact and may allow a partner to face a problem without interference. Simply listening, or making a phone call, or giving a card may help to bolster your partner's strength. No fixing is possible, but quiet loving contact does help.

Tell about a time when you wanted to give up your own well-being for someone who was not taking care of him- or herself.

. . . make room for our own beliefs . . .

We are individuals who have joined our lives to make a partnership. Our partnership is stronger when we bring to it our individuality and our unique gifts. Sometimes we feel tempted to put our own thoughts or wishes aside and to think only of what our partner thinks, wants, or needs. But if we fail to make room for our own beliefs, wishes, and needs, we cannot carry out our half of the partnership. Of course, we must be able to compromise and seek each other's pleasure. But when we fail to share our own view or seek our individual expression, there is nothing to compromise, no joining of our separate strengths, no working through to the best choice, because we have only half of the ingredients for the recipe.

Tell your partner one way you know you are different from him or her.

. . . just let our partner know we are here . . .

It is hard to let someone we love face a challenge. We want to save and protect that person from harm. Sometimes we think that we are better equipped, that we can see the dangers better, take the test, or even accept the blows to our self-esteem better than our partner can. But a respectful relationship has no room for that sort of protection.

One of the most respectful and difficult things we must do is quietly let our partner meet challenges on her or his own. At those times we face our powerlessness to fix everything. It takes inner security simply to be a cheerleader and just let our partner know we are here and that we care. This is immensely helpful. In that role we stay out of the way and let our partner walk his or her own path of personal growth.

Name a situation in which you tried to fight your partner's battles instead of supporting your partner to fight her or his own.

*. . . put our efforts where
we can succeed.*

The appeal of a "fix" tempts us. One day we dream, "If only I had a different job my life would be happy, or If only I had a different house." Perhaps we even dream of having a different partner. When we waste so much precious energy on trying to change something or someone outside ourselves, we usually end up alone, unhappy, or exhausted. It takes great effort and a long time to develop what we truly seek: love, self-acceptance, honesty, and peace of mind.

Fixing or changing our partner might appeal on the surface, but why not put our efforts where we can succeed? What can we change? Ourselves. By becoming less critical we build our honesty and self-worth. Do I block my own growth when I focus on someone else's actions?

*Name a "fix" that tempted
or distracted you in the past.*

*. . . getting back to the art
and spirit of intimacy . . .*

Sometimes we feel so pressured coping with life that we have little energy or time left over to notice and enjoy each other. These times might come during a period of high stress at work, when a child's needs take first priority, or on an extended visit with in-laws. The art and spirit of intimacy sometimes require us to pass through the flatland without getting lost there, and return again to our close rapport.

There is a danger that we can somehow get so used to coping with stress and demands that we don't find our way back to the nourishment of touch, eye contact, and private talk with our partner. We may wake up one day and realize that we feel more like roommates or brother and sister than a couple who are life partners. As if a spell had been cast, we sense the unnecessary distance between us, and we feel neglected or uncared for. The first words that express this feeling and break the spell may bring anger and an argument. But words expressed with strong feelings provide a passageway back to intimacy.

*Tell your partner how you honestly feel
right now about your connection.*

DIFFERENCES

. . . not just because we are alike . . .

Opposites and contrasts are universal—we cannot have pleasure without pain, relaxation without stress, sunshine without rain, birth without death. When we try to control these universal contrasts, we waste energy and only increase our difficulties. While our similarities provide easy understanding and bridges, our contrasts and differences can create ways to give to each other and learn.

If we are right-handed, that does not make our left hand worthless. We may naturally reach first with our dominant hand, but our other hand is still vital. When a man says, "Women are nothing but trouble," he not only puts down half the human race, but himself too, because within him lies his valuable female side. When a woman says, "Men are all jerks," she rejects the masculine side of her nature. The differences between us challenge us, although we are sometimes tempted to control them or suppress them. We love each other not just because we are alike, but because we are different. Our contrasts go together like stars against the night sky; one is invisible without the other.

Name a quality in your partner that you admire and that contrasts with you.

. . . to develop a sense of respect
for our differences.

Habits, mannerisms, and quirks of personality
in our partner sometimes aggravate us. Some of
these things we can accommodate, some we can
change, and others seem to be locked in place. We
may feel that we have to choose between accommodating our partner or steadfastly trying to
change him or her. Yet all the preaching and cajol-
ing in the world will not bring about change, and
we may not care to be accommodating. Then perhaps we can try to be respectful of both our partner's style and our own. We can take care of our
own needs and not judge our partner.

It is important to develop a sense of respect for
our differences. Respecting a partner's style does
not mean we must always accommodate it. Some
compromise is important, but we can still respect
our individual needs.

Choose something about your mate that
aggravates you; then imagine simply
respecting your differences.

Every conflict has many levels.

Some couples live as if they were fighting a cold war. Conflicts are handled by retreat into silence with each feeling like a self-righteous victim. When we retreat into this role we abandon ourselves and our commitments to our relationship. We tear away at the relationship we originally created out of love and hope.

When conflicts arise, as they must, resolution depends on taking the risk to go back to our partner with enough calmness to listen and speak our piece. We must let go of our pride and desire to be right. We each believe our case is just. But our differences are not necessarily about who is right or wrong, good or bad. Every conflict has many levels. Many times in conflict what we want most is to feel listened to and understood. When we listen and work to understand, we can let go of our need to "win," and our differences can build our common strength.

*Tell your partner about a conflict
or difference of opinion that
you have gone silent with.*

. . . walk on the path
of profound connection.

We each have special gifts to contribute to our relationship. We have gifts for ourselves and gifts to share with our partner. One partner may like to organize and plan for the future, while the other notices the small details in what is happening here and now. One may be a dreamer who thinks of creative ideas, while the other pays attention to the practical side of life. We each have our own unique style of living in and dealing with our world. When we appreciate our special gifts, we create wonderful new possibilities.

Probably we have already learned to accept some difficult realizations about ourselves and our partner. We discover that we do not always see the same meaning in our discussions with each other, or in our experiences. When we appreciate our partner's different point of view, and at the same time value our own, we walk on the path of profound connection.

Name a difference between you
and your partner and say how
it enhances your relationship.

. . . with no hidden cutting edge.

The respect and dignity a couple show each other set the table from which they are nourished for all other activities in their lives. Any feeling can be expressed in respectful or disrespectful ways. Anger is one of the most difficult to express respectfully. Everyone feels frustrated and angry at times. The crucial thing to learn is how to be angry and still be respectful—how to deal with our impatience without blame or put-downs. Many of us have to learn how to love without being possessive, how to be playful in a lighthearted way with no hidden cutting edge. When we treat our partner with disrespect, we pour poison into our own well. It may feel satisfying at first, but the long-term consequences are not good to live with.

When we are committed to respect in our relationship, we continue to learn at even deeper levels what respect truly means. We find that simply listening to each other—and letting in our differences—is a form of respect that nourishes us.

Name a difference between you and your mate that you respect.

. . . look at our differences with interest . . .

Seasoning a soup only with salt makes boring soup. The most flavorful blend contains many ingredients: herbs, vegetables, broth, maybe a little meat. If we insist that our partner be exactly like us, think alike, make decisions in the same way, or always come to the same conclusions, we will not have a partnership of two people, we will have clones. No one really wants that. We need a little pepper in the pot to keep it vital and zesty. Differences of opinion stretch us; they offer us other avenues to consider.

Think of some of the unique qualities that we enjoy in our partner and those that exasperate us. Remember, some of those exasperating ones may once have seemed charming. If we look at our differences with interest and appreciation, rather than as points to change, we find that together we create a unique and flavorful soup.

Name a facet of your partner's personality
that you have tried to change,
and find a positive quality in that trait.

. . . to provide a loving challenge.

The best relationship is not always placid and serene. We may yearn for peace and a partnership that is always comfortable and playful. But the most healthy, most creative relationships help each partner grow. Strong relationships grow when people show their strength and sometimes are willing to stand up to each other. They care, believe in each other's potential, and know each other's shortcomings. When one says, "I'm not going to apply for the promotion because it would be too hard to get," the other one says, "Oh, you can do it! It's worth the effort!"

Part of our job is to provide a loving challenge to our mate. Sometimes that means, in a sense, biting the hand that feeds us. It means saying something because it is the most honest thing to say, even when we know our mate will feel angry at first. There is love in facing our mate's anger when we tell our truth. A challenge to our partner may ignite a faith in her or him that more is possible.

Name a recent challenge
that stirred the calm waters of your
relationship for the better.

Agreement is usually not necessary.

Many of us have lived as if we always had to be right. We did not stop to notice that other things we cared about were being lost—such as friends who got tired of our persistent need to be right, or children whose self-esteem was undermined when there was no room for their ideas, or a former mate who drifted away because we could relax only if we were proven right. In our differences there is much more to look at and far more to settle than who is right and who is wrong.

An intimate connection is simply communicating our differences to each other and understanding them. Agreement is usually not necessary. Our partnership gives us an opportunity to view the world intimately through someone else's eyes. Defeating our differences defeats our opportunities to learn. We need just exclaim, "Oh, that's another way to see it!" Our task is to learn how our partner sees the world. We grow because we gain a second outlook.

Describe a difference of opinion
that has enlarged your understanding.

CHANGE

Life is what happens along the way.

We began our committed relationship with dreams and plans for the future. But all dreams and most plans get changed. Something comes along—perhaps an unplanned pregnancy, the loss of a job, a conflict at work, the death of a friend or family member. Suddenly, change forces us to adjust to unforeseen events.

Imagine sitting in an airplane on the runway, ready to take off when the pilot announces that mechanical problems have forced our flight to be canceled. We must choose a different way. Perhaps we drive. The scenery is different, the road is bumpy in places, there may be a detour or two, and our trip takes more time than we planned. But eventually we reach our destination. Life is more than just arriving at goals and fulfilling our expectations. Most of life is what happens along the way to our destination. We make adjustments, grow wiser by dealing with our challenges, learn to enjoy the road, notice the scenery, and take in events as they happen.

Tell your partner
about a recent frustration.
Have you found the reward in it yet?

Who has a right to teach?

Teachers often say how much they learn about a subject by teaching it. In our closest relationships we sometimes give little lessons to our partner and suddenly realize that we are not practicing what we preach. That naturally raises a sore point with the partnership. One might say to the other, "Who are you to talk? Look at yourself first!"

The issue of who needs to learn and who has a right to teach is inevitable between couples. These encounters help define the boundaries between us. In any equal relationship, teaching with our partner's invitation is a friendly gift, and without it is an unfair intrusion.

Tell your partner what you would most like to learn from her or him.

We learn to expect the unexpected.

Serenity and satisfaction come not when we achieve some measure of precarious temporary control, but when we learn to expect the unexpected. They come when we learn the art of responding to change and accommodating the ever-shifting circumstances of our lives. We did not choose our journey before we were born. We did not choose the fact that this journey will end in death. Naturally we want to control what we can, and our lives are better when we do so. But the best part of the adventure comes in taking what life brings to us and learning how to make it work. No amount of blaming, criticism, soul-searching, or grumpiness will ever unearth the reasons why changes happen. Our relationship can be corroded by the acid of blame, but it becomes stronger when we join together as a team to cope with the events that shape our lives.

Tell your partner one event in your relationship that you did not welcome but that brought new growth.

We must continuously
fine-tune our bearings.

No one can set sail and expect to forget the wind. First you stand in the open air, feel the wind touch your face, and take note of its direction and force. Then you set your sail to carry your boat toward your goal. And you continue to recheck the wind because it is ever-changing.

We might wish we could nail down our achievements when we finally reach them, stop the march of time, or keep our loved ones safe where they are. Just when we think we have everything together, something changes. Children grow up, jobs change, new neighbors move in next door. Like a sailor, we must continuously fine-tune our life bearings. Whether a change is welcome or not, we must respond. Our main choice is not what will change but *how we respond*. If we hold too tightly to willful thinking, we are not attuned. But if we make peace with change, we grow. We will be transformed into more than we could ever imagine.

Name the change you
are most aware of today.

*Spiritual growth
requires letting go.*

If we came out of childhood feeling unsafe, inadequate, or overly alert to the next crisis, we also learned ways to cope that made us feel better. Some of those ways of coping might now stall our growth or hinder our ability to be intimate with our partner. We need to loosen our grasp on those old ways of coping. Always reacting to secure our safety and never taking risks will block the development of a comfortable intimacy. We can never fulfill the childhood dream of an absolutely reliable partner or a life free of mishaps. We do not need to stop seeking security, but we know its rewards are too limited for us to have a satisfying life.

When, in spite of ourselves, we hold too tightly to fears and old ways of coping, we will get better at only one thing: assuring our safety. Spiritual growth requires the grown-up skills of letting go and taking risks to become more intimate.

*Name a childhood fear or pain
that you have left behind.*

We have vitally important work . . .

This is an important day. It is one of the limited number of days we are granted. We have vitally important work to develop ourselves as human beings, grow in our relationships, and contribute to the well-being of other people. Each moment's choice may be small, but it creates a direction for the moment that follows. Each act has consequences.

Perhaps we say, "I can't live like I choose today because of all the demands on my time. I have so many things to do! I can only keep putting one foot in front of the other." Throughout life, we usually have little choice about the demands we face. But we do have a choice about what kind of person we will be and how we will face the demands. The temptation to discard this day, or to numb our mindfulness, or to grab for control will lead to frustration and despair. We can live today the way we want to live our whole life.

Make a choice now for the attitude
you will bring to the demands of today.

A problem can ultimately bring us a gift.

We start our relationship in excitement, hope, and good feelings, with perhaps a measure of fear mixed in. Our history is yet to evolve. A beginning is more a time of romance than reality. But no lasting connection is built on a steady string of good times. Relationships deepen the way individuals do—by meeting the hard times, not accepting defeat, and using difficulty to learn and grow. That is how a problem, something we do not want or choose in our lives, can ultimately bring us a gift.

One year the biggest problem a couple dealt with was illness, another year it was a financial pinch, and another year almost everything came easily. Each situation called for new responses from within, yet for the same spiritual attitude of living one day at a time. Looking back, they appreciate the richness of their lives together because they have risen above their problems, grown from them, and had many times of fun and pleasure. Their problems were hard but built their relationship.

Describe a problem that turned out to be a gift for you.

. . . we stay open to surprises.

In the midst of change we reach a point of knowing that we can never go back to the way things used to be. The past is dead, but moving forward has risks. At least we knew what to expect with our old life; the future is unpredictable. Life may have been chaotic—maybe we felt bad about ourselves, maybe our survival seemed to hinge on controlling our mate or controlling our own feelings. We may have felt pain but it was a familiar pain, not the insecurity of newness and the unknown.

This process of change will carry us toward better lives if we stay open to surprises. We cannot know what change will create. We have to tolerate some unfamiliar feelings, but we can ride our feelings through to the other side, where new and better ways become familiar. Telling our fears to each other diminishes their power to immobilize us and keeps doors open to progress.

Tell your partner your fears about changes in your lives and how you deal with them.

Sharing some of the struggles.

The day her father died she thought that the world had come to an end, that nothing would ever be the same. The grief she felt in the first year after he died was painful. She was angry at his leaving her, angry that she never really knew him, and she blamed him for that. Sharing some of the struggle of letting go of her father deepened her connection to her partner.

We all have experienced the loss of loved ones: some through death, some through divorce or a career move, and others in different ways. How do we carry on when we must say good-bye to a relationship that was meaningful? Some of us want to withdraw; others reach out to loved ones for comfort; still others escape by immersing themselves in addictive behavior.

Recalling good and bad memories helps our healing. No one is a perfect angel or a perfect monster. By remembering our lost loved ones and talking about them, we claim their gifts to us—both the good and the not-so-good. In life and in death a connection always remains that nothing can erase.

Name a gift from someone whose absence you grieve.

*. . . the living touch
of another human being.*

When tragedy strikes, we fight to understand why. Something may strike out of nowhere and turn our lives around. We would like to believe that there is some way to explain tragedy. We think that if we could explain it, maybe we could protect ourselves. We wonder if we are being punished. Has an uncaring God abandoned us? We may believe that if God cared, no tragedy would happen.

This is not always a just world. But if we let God be there for us, listening to our rage at injustice and comforting our tears, we can recover, move on, and know that we are not alone. God is with us in the words and the living touch of another human being. We may want to retreat within ourselves when tragedy strikes. This is not a bad or wrong feeling, but it is still important to let others be with us. Time spent with friends and family, and prayer time with our Higher Power, help us realize that we are not alone in our grief.

*Remember a painful time
and tell your partner what helped
you get through it.*

*Our problem is that we expect
to feel secure.*

Many of us have had past crises and problems,
yet our worries and anxieties continue in the present. We believe that our situation causes our fears
and we say, "If only things were different, I could
relax." Yet even when everything is going well, we
still get anxious that something unseen is amiss.
When we are immersed in our fears, unable to let
go and live life joyfully, we may become emotionally absent from our loved ones.

Our problem is not that life is insecure. Of
course it is. Our problem is that we expect to feel
secure. We put great energy into achieving control
and having everything "just right," but quite naturally we end up without control. Then we think
something is wrong. Instead, we can choose to
turn our fears over to our Higher Power. We do
that by talking about our fears, taking the steps we
can, and trusting our Higher Power for the outcomes. Then we return to emotional contact in our
relationship.

*Tell your partner something you fear
and turn it over to your
Higher Power.*

*. . . our ordinary lives
become courageous.*

Courage means we do not waste precious energy on self-pity. Instead, we get on with living. We might wish we could always live a certain way, or we think we should. Since we do not, we might think it is our own fault, we might brood about our difficult lot, or we might blame others. Looking at neighbors or people we admire we may say, "Their life is so easy. They do everything right. Why can't I be like them?"

Many courageous people, thinking back on their moment of greatest courage, have said, "I just did what I had to do." In truth, no one lives an entire life without problems and times of serious challenge. We do not choose when problems come and how they come. But we do choose how we meet our difficulties, how we respond to pain or trouble. And when we stop wasting energy on *poor me* and *bad me* thoughts, our ordinary lives become courageous. Then we use our difficulties to learn new truths, to bring forth our best qualities and our greatest strengths.

*Name one problem in your life today.
Can you see how you might
use it to grow?*

. . . accept it as a wise teacher.

A couple has a child whom they would go to great lengths to protect, yet the child falls ill and lies near death. A woman devotes years to a career; then the economy shifts, leaving her unemployed. Addiction diverts a man from his path, and he loses everything he cares about. Life brings trial and defeat as part of its package. We would never choose defeat and we cannot avoid its pain, but we can accept it as a wise teacher. Out of defeat is born new strength.

As a couple we need wisdom to deal with defeat and grief. We will face them together more than once. The false comforts of self-pity and blame may tempt us in our pain, but they take much more from us than they give back. Through crisis we see clearly what truly counts in our lives, and we are better prepared to relish the pleasures when they arrive.

*Name a defeat that you
faced together.*

. . . we are never alone.

We know adversity comes to all. We know it changes us as it passes through. The question is, how will we change in its wake? When we cannot prevail, will we become embittered and beaten, or will we become wiser and more loving? Adversity makes equals of us all. We may grow and deepen together through adversity, or we may become more tense and strained. We have choices in how we will change.

We hope fate will treat us well. We hope the storm that challenges us will be light and pass quickly. But when stress and difficulty overtake us, we are never alone. Our Higher Power guides and befriends us. Sometimes the trouble is more difficult for one of us than for the other. But when we continue to talk openly about our thoughts and feelings, both of us become stronger than either would be in silence.

Name a current problem
and say how you feel about it.

. . . our problem teaches us.

Some of the most gifted geniuses said that their inventions came after they were stumped by their logic. They got nowhere when they applied all the force of rational solutions to a problem. That was the necessary beginning. Then a burst of insight leaped around their logic. Some said it came as a dream while they slept; others described visual images that seemed to pop into their minds when they relaxed.

As couples we sometimes face a life problem that doesn't have answers. We wish we had more money to pay our bills, we yearn for our child to be free of a problem, or prejudice continues to frustrate our lives. Life is not always fair, and we may face a cruel injustice or a frustrating riddle that we can't fix or make disappear. So together we live with it. Although we can't change our problem, in the course of time it changes us and teaches us something. Insight grows within us and leads us into realms of understanding and acceptance that our logical answers could not.

Make room for insight in your life
by resting, relaxing,
and playing.

WE ARE ONLY HUMAN

We can admit our limitations and defects.

When we admit the truth about our limitations and defects, we create fertile ground for new growth and change. But if we wallow in hopeless belief that our defects are just our true nature, we grow committed to them. That is the difference between powerlessness and helplessness. When we accept our powerlessness to control everything, we wake up to a deeper wisdom: that more willfulness only brings more defeat. Some of our needs can only be met and some growth can only happen when we receive a healing infusion of outside help.

But when we tenaciously refuse to accept our powerlessness, our dogged willfulness keeps us trying harder to do what we cannot do alone. Eventually that leads to resignation and helplessness. Our better choice is both painful and hopeful. We can admit our limitations and defects. Then we become receptive to help and acceptance from our mate, other people and from our Higher Power.

Tell your partner one of your defects
that you are willing
to give up.

. . . to continue to do our best . . .

We cannot ever completely understand life. What seems totally bad at first later turns out to have a good side: out of our weaknesses we find strength, out of grief comes freedom, out of letting go comes serenity. We do not fully understand these paradoxes, but they give us a taste of life's mystery.

Pain brings us out of childhood innocence into adult knowing. Perhaps in our innocence we thought that if we worked hard and did what was right our lives would go well, but along came a random accident, an illness, a serious disagreement that we could not fix. Then, no matter how hard we worked, life seemed painful and in disarray. Out of pain an inner voice called to us and asked us to continue to do our best, to take the risk of reaching for what we honor most, to see our common bond with all who struggle. So we grew to become bigger persons than we could ever have been in our innocence. We exchange our childhood simplicity for a more grown-up acceptance that life is full of mystery, and we learn courage and strength to meet it.

*Name a problem
that brought out the best in you.*

*. . . paying attention
to our own growth.*

Trusting our partner has a lot to do with trusting ourselves. When we feel confused, unsure, or in conflict about our own direction, we may shift our attention outside ourselves. Even when we feel unsure about our self-worth, our negative feelings may crystalize as blame directed toward someone else.

Looking outward in that negative way and avoiding responsibility for ourselves makes liars of us. When we do that we are not paying attention to our own growth, not looking at the truth. If we do not claim ownership of our part in a conflict, we will not be able to trust our partner either. We build trust when we are honest with ourselves and expose our truth and vulnerability to our mate.

*Tell your partner something you trust
about her or him.*

. . . dare to open up to each other . . .

With the power in our muscles we can lift a heavy appliance or force open a jammed door. In an intimate relationship a different kind of strength helps us dare to open up to each other and dare to let another know us. When we move toward each other in partnership, we become more vulnerable because we give up some defenses.

As our partner gets to know us better, he or she sees our weaknesses and knows what makes us happy or loving or angry. To be understood can make us feel less lonely, more connected with each other. And when we know our partner's vulnerability and unattractive side, our strength is in holding that in trust, being respectful of the keys our partner has given us.

*Name one way you know you can
please your partner, and one way
you know you can get him or her angry.*

*. . . after conflict
a special understanding . . .*

Any two people living with each other will step on each other's feet from time to time. No matter how much love we feel, no matter how romantic our beginnings, still we must work out ways to share our space and express our personalities. We need to agree on how much to intrude into each other's affairs, and we need to find ways we can give and receive without becoming defensive. The comfort and pleasure we felt at the beginning of a relationship may pass through periods of tension and conflict as we face the complexities of increased sharing. But after the conflict may come a special understanding, unique to us, that comes from knowing and accepting each other more deeply.

*Ask your partner if he or she feels
comfortable with how space
is shared in your relationship.*

Our human right to feel bad . . .

The writings of ancient prophets teach wisdom gleaned, not just from one wise person's life, but from many generations of human struggle, learning, and insight. They help us learn how to be better human beings. We may have once thought we had to be perfect, fully developed, and untarnished in order to be acceptable. Perhaps we think that feeling weak, inadequate, or empty are bad feelings that we should get rid of.

Many old writings of mythology, spiritual wisdom, and scripture say do not fight the truth. They say to accept all of our feelings as part of being human and we will be more complete. It is in standing up for our human right to feel bad that we begin to feel better. It is in acknowledging we made a mistake that we get ready to make a repair. Out of weakness comes true strength.

*Tell your mate about a weakness of yours
that turned into a strength.*

. . . meet them head-on
with humility.

When we do something that hurts our partner or violates our values, we may first want to talk ourselves out of feeling bad. When we come up against our mistakes and guilt, it never helps to compare ourselves with the evils of a tyrant or the goodness of a saint. True humility means knowing we are human, neither purely good nor utterly bad but somewhere in the middle. By facing our flaws and mistakes honestly, we can give ourselves permission to act better in the future.

In admitting our mistakes and hearing our partner's guilt when he or she makes a mistake, we face the truth between us and allow for change. This process can be frightening and at the same time renewing. The truth is that mistakes hurt a relationship more when they are hidden or distorted. When we meet them head-on with humility, we can use them as stepping stones for learning and change.

Choose one action today
that you will measure with humility,
not with the yardstick of a saint or a devil.

Healing is ongoing.

We often think of healing as a special process that occurs after an injury or after a rift in our relationship. Actually, healing goes on all the time in our lives. We normally need ample doses of it every day to stay strong and healthy. Just as we know that housework is never done, and the gas tank seems to always need a refill, our mind and body always benefit from healing and uplifting experiences. To speak a few words to our partner about what we appreciate in him or her, to prepare a favorite meal to please her or him, to spend a quiet evening together relaxing and listening to music— these and many other healing experiences keep our partnership whole and strong.

The healing process takes time to ripen, and we can block it if we become willful. Impatiently demanding an apology when we think we deserve one or insisting on a talk based on our feeling of need and our time schedule may produce a power struggle instead of the healing we yearn for. The natural healing process continues freely when we trust it and set aside our willfulness.

*Name a healing experience
you had recently.*

The rules we grew up with . . .

Most of us come to a committed relationship with a set of "shoulds" that we inherited from our parents. Our partner brings his or her "shoulds" too. As we put them together we are presented with a question, Whose rules and whose needs will we live by? Sometimes, in ridding ourselves of the "shoulds" of the past, we create their opposites. For instance, if an old rule demanded neatness and order, we might deliberately choose to leave things more messy. Or we might think that instead of pleasing our parents, we must now please our mate. But when we choose only between these "shoulds," we still do not have our own inner values and preferences to help us weigh and choose wisely.

When we understand the rules we grew up with, we can make better choices for ourselves. When we develop our inner voice, and communicate with our partner so that we hear both voices, our partnership grows and flourishes.

Talk with your partner
about some of the "shoulds"
that pull you in two directions.

Reflecting on where we have been . . .

Many of us have been through a great deal, both as individuals and as couples. We know that reflecting on where we have been is helpful. Sometimes we feel that we have not made any progress because we still get into the same old fights. But let's be realistic and look at what we have learned. We are probably better at noticing when we are off-track. Knowing that gives us the power to name the problem and work on it.

Perfectionism never got us anywhere before, and it surely won't get us anywhere now. Our spirit and our energy brought us this far. We can value our spirit and celebrate it!

Talk with your mate
and name areas of progress
you have made in your relationship.

> . . . we live several lives
> in one lifetime.

Waking up from a terrifying dream, we first sigh with deep relief, "Thank God it was just a dream." After we have made a big mistake in real life we long for the chance to undo it. We do not get to undo those moments, but life is still full of second chances . . . and third and fourth chances. The big question is, Do we learn from our experiences?

In some ways, we live several lives in one lifetime and we have several phases in one relationship. Today is a new day, and it presents all the possibilities of a new beginning. We have learned from the past. As painful and difficult as our experiences were, we can feel stronger today because we have learned from them. Injustice and fateful accidents can befall anyone. Yet many difficult times never need to be repeated. Today we can be grateful for another day with all the new opportunities it brings.

> Name one way you are
> different today because of what
> you have learned from your experience.

. . . learn it in small steps.

Some of us want to forget our past. We want to forget that we were married before, or that we were abused, or that we did things we regret. We justify our denial with phrases like, "You can't live in the past!" Hard times are valuable teachers, but if we refuse to remember them and talk about them we cannot learn their lessons. Instead of growing wiser, stronger, deeper, those who refuse to remember simply keep starting over again, never building on the past.

Building on the past may be difficult. We can learn it in small steps. We can begin by talking about an event in our past. Who have we talked to about the event? What did it mean to us? How do we feel about it today? We can talk about anything if we just find a way to say it. Then it loses its power to harm us, and we can grow from it.

Tell your mate one memory, happy or sad, from the time before you met each other. What did that memory mean to you?

. . . part of the great woven fabric . . .

Mending is a good metaphor for daily spiritual life. We are each part of the great woven fabric of the world community. When a couple in their mud brick house in Africa maintains a just and joyful relationship, the world is a little bit better place because of them. But only they can control themselves and their relationship, and that is true for each of us, wherever we are.

We return daily—not to perfection, but to our mending. We reach into that mending bag and pull out a needle and thread to repair the rip or snag created by our selfishness, thoughtlessness, or dishonesty. We are valuable members of the human community when we take our own moral inventory and make daily repairs for our mistakes.

Tell your partner something
you will mend today.

We learn from making mistakes and repairing them.

We do not believe in perfection, we believe in mending. We make progress toward a goal, but we seldom move in a straight line toward it without missteps. Life is like a zigzag chain of events that first brings everything together just as we want and then spills it all over again. We try to do our best, but inevitably we make mistakes. So a large part of normal daily life is spent mending.

When we accept imperfection as a fact of life, we make peace with the constant need for repairs. Saying "I made a mistake and I owe you an apology" is never fun, but when we do it we grow stronger. Every disappointment, every complaint, points to an underlying hope or wish. We can use them to point us to repairs we would like to make. We do not learn anything new from correctly repeating what we already know. We learn from making mistakes and repairing them.

Select one complaint or one mistake that you want to mend and turn into a learning experience.

. . . the only way for love to stay vital.

Any relationship has some regrets and painful memories to look back on. Many couples see clearly now what was cloudy and obscure before. Some groan, "We got together for all the wrong reasons," or "There were too many strikes against us!" Yet for all couples the passage of time will bring some regrets. Facing problems with the wisdom of hindsight is no reason to discard a relationship. It is the only way for love to stay vital.

We might get discouraged looking back and seeing so clearly the problems we had. But the real question today is, Can we learn from them? If we can learn, we will become stronger, wiser, and more joyful people than if we had lived a less trying, less troubled life. A healed break is often stronger than the original bond.

Name a difficult time that you worked through and the gifts your relationship received as a result.

There is no total answer.

Studying and reading are traditional methods of spiritual growth. With a lifelong routine of study each day, a person or couple grows under the guidance of the sages. Civilization exists because each generation builds upon the progress of the past. We do not have to reinvent the wheel. After we learn from those who have gone before, we may even discover and create beyond the point where they left off. But if we are in a willful, defiant mood, we may say, "I have to find my own way. I don't feel like learning from anyone." Our individualism then becomes a half-truth, silently trapping us in problems that others have found answers to.

There is no total answer—no total freedom—only continued growth. Daily reading, openness to learn from others' encounters with life, and study of how they faced their most challenging spiritual questions will bring us progress.

Name a spiritual writing
you find helpful.

To know our mate
in this new day . . .

Some of us have lived through the anguish of divorce. We all have echoes of past hurts from divorce or other events that can still threaten our ability to trust and hope. Some of us hear the voice of an overly critical father or an overly protective mother when our partner speaks. Or we hear the voices of parents who fought too much in our own raised voices. Today we might be supersensitive with our mate, as if the same old scenes were about to be replayed.

Wisdom teaches us that no mate can erase or totally avoid our old wounds. Sometimes we have to remind ourselves that our mate is not our ex-spouse, father, or mother. Our memories define the past, not the present, situation. When we let go of the past, we are freed to know our mate as he or she is in this new day of our lives.

Name a behavior in your mate
you are oversensitive to.

*To stop yielding
to our reactive impulses . . .*

When a friend makes remarks about a sensitive
subject, we might rise to the bait and say things we
do not really mean. When a spouse does not take
good care of her- or himself, we may get so
involved in the problem that we neglect our own
needs. Someone else's behavior might get us so
mad that we violate our ethics just to get revenge.

To stop yielding to our reactive impulses is a
high mountain to climb. Those who do not climb
their mountain stay trapped in the slavery of reac-
tion. Every time we react to a trigger we go off on
another tangent and say or do things that diminish
our self-esteem. To avoid reacting this way, we can
first reduce our stress level by quietly meditating
every day, getting plenty of rest, being honest with
ourselves, having friends with whom we can talk
openly, and developing a conscious relationship
with our Higher Power. As with learning to paint a
fine picture, time and persistent effort will develop
our skill. The reward is a life filled with inner
strength and self-respect.

*Name a situation that tempts you
to react rather than act out of
your inner guidance.*

. . . humility lets us empathize . . .

Many of us once thought that humility meant almost the same as humiliation. But a loving relationship teaches us what mature humility is. That is an attitude that says, "I like and respect myself and I expect you to like and respect me even though I am not the center of the universe. I have a place in the family of God, but I am not complete within myself. I can't do everything; I don't know everything; I need to listen to others and I need others to listen to me."

Imperfection and mistakes are natural. When we lovingly accept our mistakes and make amends for them, we become more forgiving of others. Constantly thinking about how bad we are or how unworthy we are is a form of self-centeredness. Mature humility frees us from those bonds and lets us empathize with each other.

*Name one of your imperfections
you have learned to accept.*

ORDINARY MOMENTS

Ordinary moments created
a real relationship. . . .

Today may be an ordinary day, not a big turning point like the day you graduated from high school or the day you first met the person who would become your life partner. Take a moment now to recall some past ordinary days. Remember waking up with your partner on a lazy weekend morning. Remember driving to visit relatives. Remember going to the movies. These ordinary moments when you were just going about the business of living were the stuff that created a real relationship. Today is part of that stuff. You can choose what qualities you want to give your relationship today. You might create a sense of beauty by playing some favorite music, or bring forth the feeling of intimacy by raising a discussion of your inner thoughts, or get active in a game of tennis or a brisk walk together.

The spiritual life of a relationship takes form in the way we live our ordinary days. Only a few turning points come along in a lifetime. The real building blocks are these ordinary days.

Tell your partner what you would choose
to influence the flavor of your relationship
today.

Changes create renewed interest.

When we move the furniture in a room, the room itself may seem to change. Perhaps it feels larger, more open, more inviting. Furnishings we looked past without seeing now stand out. These changes are refreshing and create renewed interest. Just as we need to move the furniture in our home occasionally, from time to time we need to rearrange the furniture in our heart and mind.

Sometimes change is forced on us by a new job, someone's illness, or the needs of growing children. After we get past our resentment of being forced, we realize that good things come from it. Other times we can choose new experiences that refresh our outlook. For example, if we do household chores every Saturday morning, we might change the routine and take a Saturday morning for an outing together. Or we can trade routine household tasks, give our partner a gift even though it's not a birthday, go see a matinee, or read a poem out loud.

Name one change in your partner
that reignited your interest
in him or her.

How are you doing?
How am I doing?

Just as the ivy that grows on a windowsill requires water and light, our friendships need care and nourishment. We might wish that a good friend would be there whenever we wanted. But we get so busy scrambling to cover all the bases in our lives that we lose touch with friends, even with our partner. We neglect even to ask, How are you doing? How am I doing?

In spite of our busyness, the time we take for a brief telephone call can make us feel more relaxed and less busy. These seemingly small attentions are important to friendships and instill the spirit of human warmth and care into our lives. It reminds us again of what gives us meaning and opens us up to the affectionate feelings in our partnership.

Call a friend you have not seen for a while just to renew your connection.

. . . attention to each little moment . . .

Our lives take shape not just in the dramatic
moments of profound change or when we take bold
action, but also in the ordinariness of our daily
routines. In these routines we build continuity,
trust, and faithfulness. Standing at the cutting
board chopping celery for tonight's dinner, walking
to the mailbox to send off this month's payment
for the water bill, stopping for a period of quiet
reflection, we carry on these necessary tasks that
make our lives possible.

Hidden within those mundane moments are
spiritual truths that can nourish our lives.
Appreciating the details of color and scent, breathing the fresh air, creating order in our lives—
through these we initiate and communicate with
our Higher Power. Spiritual aliveness does not
come from the excitement around us. It flows into
us through an inner wellspring of attention to each
little moment and gives each moment its place in
our lives.

*Become alert right
now and describe for your
partner what your senses are taking in.*

. . . we live on more than one level.

Most days do not feel like great spiritual experiences—they feel like just another day. In fact, some days seem filled with the same old thing—boredom and drudgery. But we are more than what we do. We carry the spark of our creator within us and we live on more than one level at a time. While going through the same traffic to work today, or going through all the routines of our lives, we are also connected with our Higher Power.

One form of prayer or meditation is to use our routines to become conscious of and open to our Higher Power. While mowing the grass, doing aerobics, or bathing, we can also maintain conscious contact with God. Then these moments are not just drudgery, because on another level we are in touch with the fire of our being.

Sit quietly. Close your eyes.
Do not try to do anything.
Feel the spark of life moving within you.

Make the whole day
rich and satisfying . . .

We want our lives to mean something, to add up to something. We want to feel that each day leads to worthwhile goals. It might seem strange then to say, "Keep it simple." But simplicity and greatness often travel the same path. For example, the beauty of Greek architecture has moved humanity's soul for twenty-five hundred years, yet is founded on simple lines. And the Golden Rule's simple message, "Do unto others as you would have them do unto you," is a part of all great world religions.

In our lives together, we can say or do simple things that make living rich and satisfying. There is no need for excess. Simply sitting down to share a meal together each day, perhaps lighting a candle during mealtime, telling a joke, going for a walk, making eye contact for a moment, cuddling together in bed before falling asleep, cleaning the house together, or saying a prayer together may fulfill our longing for something more.

Tell your partner a simple action in your daily routine that you especially like, or choose one together you would like to share.

*. . . setting aside our carefulness
with each other . . .*

If we cannot tolerate our mistakes, we will never be able to move on from this place. If we do not step up to the plate with bat in hand, we will grow old without knowing what first base is like.

Life is a risk. A committed relationship is a risk. Letting ourselves go, voicing opinions, telling our deepest feelings, playing frivolously at the park, setting aside our carefulness with each other and sometimes falling flat on our faces—all these things give us the pleasure of being alive. If we insist on playing it safe, then we never feel the thrill of the game. Our lives with each other become flat and empty if we do not take some risks. We have a right to be weak as well as strong; a right to be respected when we feel silly as much as when we appear dignified; a right to say what we believe even if it is half-baked. The greatest mistake is never to engage life.

*Think of one thing you would like to do
with your partner if you could set aside
all judgments and evaluations.*

Other choices are possible . . .

Conflict with co-workers, a partner who is pre-occupied with a problem, a child who is misbehaving—when these things happen we may feel overwhelmed and upset. Perhaps we say, "If only he would get his act together and stop causing so much trouble we would have more peace." Life is always easier when no one else is making waves. But something is always in disarray. If we let circumstances dictate our inner peace we will feel on edge most of the time.

Obsessing about another's behavior and problems is a choice we make. Other choices are possible if we stop to consider them. Listening and caring are necessary in an intimate relationship, but we become less helpful when we throw our own serenity out the window. Prayerful thought and attention to our positive connections prevent us from bogging down when others are in a difficult place.

Talk with your partner
about stresses you each encounter.
Say what you can do to nourish your spirit.

*Forget the demands
and distractions . . .*

Moments when all awareness of time falls away are spiritual moments. They nourish our relationship and our soul. We need these moments every day, not just on vacation. We get them by scheduling times to forget time. Ten minutes or half an hour of quiet will do. Shielding ourselves from distractions, putting other responsibilities aside, we let go of all burdens in our mind. They will get attention later.

Awareness of the ancient rhythms we share with our partner—the rhythms of our breathing, the ebb and flow of waking and sleeping, of hunger and meal time, of lovemaking and work—is a form of meditation. These rhythms bring us to a peaceful union. For this moment, forget the demands and distractions that tug on our lives, and remember the ancient rhythms we share with ancestors. Our lives will fit into a larger perspective, and we will feel peaceful.

*Take a few minutes now
to become quiet on the inside.*

. . . we can still feel calm.

Stress might pervade our surroundings, but we can still feel calm. Tension from problems in a relationship, from too many bills and too little money, from car problems, from worrying about our children, from conflict with relatives—these are a part of life but are not part of our core. With serenity we still have difficulties or pain, but our problems do not consume us.

Detachment is a key idea for dealing with problems. It helps us become healthier by allowing us to distinguish problems around us from problems within us. We can cope with all of them better when we separate ourselves from the problems around us. We create a hell in our mind when we lose that detachment. When we see clearly the difference between those things we can change and those we cannot, we do not add chaos to situations we cannot control.

Name a problem you have taken inside you that you could leave outside.

Mindfulness puts us squarely in the present.

Today might be one of those days that seem especially hard, even to the point of saying we will be glad when it is over. Or perhaps we feel too busy to stop and notice the day. Maybe we lean so heavily on a happy future or regretful past that today seems like a throwaway. Playing mind games with time will dry up our vital energy.

We do not have to be victims of time. Mindfulness is an attitude that puts us squarely in the present and makes us pay attention to our senses: smell, sight, touch, hearing, and taste. Mindful of what we sense, we move slowly to truly notice and enjoy what is around us. In conversation we stop to hear and be with the person speaking to us. A day is not a disposable cup to be used once and thrown away. Each day is a gift, like a cup made of fine china. We notice and appreciate it as we drink from it. It may present challenges, yet we savor it as the genuine article, never to be duplicated again, noteworthy and valuable just as it stands.

Stop. Quietly notice your breath, even the small space between breaths.

*. . . the greatest truths
in simple things.*

We feel closest to the greatest truths in the simple things. When we visit a grove of trees, a lakeshore, or a mountain, it inspires reverence. We hear the clear tones of a lone bird repeating its call; a soft gray toadstool emerges today and provides food for a woodchuck tomorrow; a tiny ant totes its burden between blades of grass. As we observe these things, our lives gain perspective, our inner resources are restored, and we become a better partner.

Simple is seeing the quiet morning light with no distraction; simple is trusting the rhythm of sunrise and sunset, appetite and satisfaction, sorrow and joy; simple is letting go of yesterday's regret and tomorrow's fear; simple is spending an hour with a true friend.

*Take a few minutes in a place
you find simplicity.*

The quiet comfort of silence . . .

Intimate partners have a kind of communion beyond words. The quiet comfort of silence strips away the distraction of words. The endless chatter of our world—intended to motivate or entertain us, or put a special spin on the truth—sometimes floods our thoughts. Beyond all that is the refuge of silence.

On the one hand, honest words can pierce the heart of our experience; on the other hand, silence can allow truth to rise to the surface. We need both. Sometimes we need to speak; other times we need silence. A tense silence can be used to cover unexpressed feelings, and until we become familiar with a calm silence we may feel unsure, as we would in any unfamiliar situation. We may want to rush to fill the void with words. When two people who are comfortable together welcome tranquil silence, they welcome another form of honesty into their lives.

Take a few minutes together
to feel the silence and tune in to it.

They bond us to each other.

We design our spiritual life by bringing beautiful moments into daily experience, noting special occasions, making a place for music, good stories, and loving friendships. By having ceremonies and rituals to mark special moments in life, we strengthen our spiritual base. Birthdays, graduations, anniversaries, farewells, weddings, funerals, new beginnings, holidays—all of these have special meaning worth marking. They bond us to each other, to our origins, to tradition, and to our ancestors. And when we mark these occasions, we are stirred deep in our soul.

We may have minimized our special moments in the past. Maybe we thought we were above sentimentality, or we did not care about the meaning of our inner lives. Now we want to live every moment fully. Now every day is an occasion worth noting. We have our lives together to celebrate. We can share a meal and appreciate what we have. Setting time aside to observe a special moment creates the opportunity for reflection and gratitude.

Plan a special moment for today.

We have our time together . . .

Sometimes we feel bad because we cannot afford all the things we need or want. Whether or not we have all we want, we can get lost in the quest for material possessions and the happiness we think they will bring.

These thoughts can carry us toward a narrow and cold view of life. But we can return to the spontaneous life that surrounds us. Squirrels still chase each other through the grass. Children still engage in fanciful conversations. The joy of music can still enrich our lives. We have our time together and our imagination. When we take the time to enjoy our connection and express our love, we discover riches of far greater value than material items.

Take this moment to look around you, to notice the simple things that give you pleasure.

Awaken to the ordinary beauty . . .

Our lives are filled with demands, responsibilities, expectations, places to go, people to see, things to do. We may get so caught up in the next task that we miss the golden moment happening right now. No matter where we are or what we are doing, if we stop to breathe slowly and notice our surroundings, we will find something to appreciate. We may see a glint of light reflecting off a pane of glass, the look in a friend's eyes, or a small thoughtful thing that our partner does.

Spiritual development is nourished by our senses. The sights, sounds, tastes, touch, and scents in our immediate surroundings are the doorway to awe and mystery. When we awaken to the ordinary beauty in our everyday lives, warm and loving parts of ourselves grow and extend out to those we love.

Quiet yourself for a moment,
slowly breathe in and out,
focus on something you appreciate.

*Saving a time
for quiet appreciation . . .*

An aesthetic life, in the broad sense, is a spiritual life. Couples can strengthen their partnership and enrich their lives by making aesthetic experiences daily events. Saving time for quiet appreciation of the good things in our lives—communicating with each other and with friends, playing and relaxing, reading to children, cooking and eating tasty, nourishing food—these are some ways to bring beauty into each day. We can also put attractive pictures and interesting things in our home to make it a place that comforts and pleases us; we can read interesting books, notice a striped caterpillar on a milkweed or the splash of stars in the night sky, relish the sensuous pleasure of a warm soapy bath, see a good movie, listen to music, grow plants.

We live spiritually when we make a place for beauty and when we slow down to enjoy the beauty that already surrounds us. We may wonder what good that may do us. The answer is that these spiritual gestures add meaning to all the other parts of our lives.

*Take a few minutes now to
appreciate something beautiful. Make
a plan to bring some beauty into this day.*

. . . they in turn enrich our lives.

Our spiritual life is on the same plane as our everyday relationships. It's not just something within our mind or feelings, and it's not just lofty and in the clouds. Spirituality is *between* people and in all *relationships*. Its growth depends on the way we relate to each other as intimate partners. We find it in our relationship to ordinary things like the bread we eat and the water we drink. Spirituality is found in the ways we honor our body with food and touch, work and rest, and in the ways we honor each other.

As a couple we jointly extend our spirituality through relationships with others. As we become friends with others or as we welcome people into our home, we receive them with hospitality because God is found in each of them. When we reach out to others or receive them as guests, they in turn enrich and bless our lives. This spiritual practice of hospitality has ancient roots all over the world. It teaches us to relate with generous hospitality to all guests who appear at our door.

Do something generous
for someone today.

. . . greater levels
of intimacy and strength . . .

Many of us emerged from a past that taught us how to survive crises and difficulty. But now we need the skills to create a life beyond surviving. We need to learn skills and habits that will take our relationship to greater levels of intimacy and strength, enhance our joy, and restore our spirits when they sag.

Beautiful things nourish life. We can create a safe and nurturing haven by hanging attractive pictures on the walls of our home, setting out special things that remind us of friends and good times, or arranging furniture in ways that feel welcoming and warm. When we arise in the morning we can start the day with a feeling of peace and beauty. Home can be a retreat that gives us pleasure, that builds our health and strength.

Name one simple way
you would like to bring more beauty
into your home.

Our lives become filled
with mystery . . .

The spirit of life and creation moves through our transitions. Some people thank God for a new day every morning when they wake up. Many people have a daily ritual of sitting quietly with a cup of coffee and meditating on the day ahead of them. Our wedding anniversary, a birthday, the day we move into a new apartment or start a new job—all have spiritual aspects that we can bring forward into the consciousness that we share. These events are occasions to marvel at the profound turns life takes.

When television entertains us every moment in private and stress and competition occupy us every day at work, we may neglect the transitions that are unique in our lives. Then we start to feel that our lives have only an outside form with no inner substance. When we mark occasions with a greeting, a gift, a meal together, or a dance, we live on the spiritual side of our humanness. Our lives become richer and filled with mystery and gratitude.

Name a date or event
that has spiritual meaning for you.

. . . the flow of our relationship.

All parts of our relationship count as part of the whole. The day we first met, the day we celebrate our anniversary, quarreling and making up, getting sick and recovering, hurting and repairing the hurt—all these may be parts of a whole picture. We may forget the whole when we become intensely involved in one piece of it. Sometimes we think a hurt we suffered or caused spoils the whole story of our partnership. Sometimes we think only the special moments count and the rest is only fluff.

But a relationship has the momentum of a river. Today we may not see every bend along the length of the river, but the entire course makes up the whole. And today's events with our mate have their place as only part in the long flow of our relationship.

Talk to your mate about important moments in your history together. What did you like about each other when you first met?

. . . flexibly unequal sometimes.

Healthy adult love relationships are flexible. They support the growth and development of both partners, yet they also allow one partner to occasionally lean on the other. When we play unequal roles of parent and child, strong and weak, or exploiter and server, we barricade our paths to further growth and begin to feel trapped by our connection rather than supported and enhanced by it.

Still, a loving partnership is flexibly unequal sometimes. When one partner is sick, he or she needs to be a receiver of care while the other is called to be the giver. If one has a big job to do, the other can be the helper. One partner might be the expert at cooking chicken, so the other plays the assistant. Our usual duties and patterns give us comfort and predictability. But when they become "shoulds," as in "You should be the cook and I should be the mechanic," or rigid demands, as in "We always did it this way so I'm not changing!" then the relationship turns stiff and lifeless.

Name a way that you are flexible
in your relationship.

. . . our dreams will lead us . . .

Big decisions are part of making a life together. Shall we move or stay where we are? Shall we have a baby? Can we start a business of our own? To find answers and make choices we will do well to tune in to our inner yearnings and desires. Notice where our quiet fantasies go. Pay close attention to our physical sensations of tightness or warmth or pleasure that come when we think about each option.

In making choices for the future we can pay close attention to what we deeply want, what will help us fulfill our hopes and our potential for a good and worthwhile life. This does not mean the same as "If it feels good do it." Many impulses are pleasurable momentarily, but fraught with consequences we would regret. Yet if we let ourselves dream about who we could be, what we could do, where we might go, our dreams will lead us to our finest selves. These are dreams that get fulfilled slowly. They may take years, but the time it takes to walk this path is worth it.

Name a lifelong wish
you have savored.

We keep our troubles
in their proper place . . .

As children we played with our sense of balance while walking on a length of board or climbing a tree. Leaning too far to one side took us out of balance; correcting too far to the other side also took us out of balance. Likewise, we need balance as we give our troubles their due without giving ourselves away to them.

Balance is a dynamic point that we maintain by constantly weighing the many forces pulling on us. We keep our troubles in their proper place, then go on to other things that also have a place. We love our child who is ill today and we give her the extra care she needs, and we love our healthy child who can go with us for a walk today in the park. We could choose to give 100 percent of our energy to our problems today, but that would probably be excessive. Native American tradition teaches us to look at today's decisions through the eyes of a person seven generations from now. That outlook puts today's problems into a balanced perspective.

Make a list of today's concerns
and decide what you can or cannot do
about them.

True love must have
a practical side.

We are inundated with images of romance that mislead us into thinking that true love means we should feel enthralled all the time. Actually, romantic love is temporary insanity. True love must have a practical side. It grows out of time spent together, sexual attraction, knowing each other well, and resolved disagreements.

If all of the images of love we brought to our partnership were learned from movies and popular music, we might feel that something was missing even when we achieved a healthy intimacy. Most of the time, this intimacy does not have the excitement of a new, intense love affair. But it has the solid assurance that someone is there when we need her or him. It brings us the joy of a partner we like to please and who likes to please us. And sometimes it challenges us with a trusted friend who will stand up to us strongly in disagreement.

Name something you like
about your partner that you learned
after the first year of your relationship.

New possibilities emerge . . .

We all have to deal with losses at some time—the tragic loss of a loved one, the painful ending of a relationship, the unplanned shift of a career. We may have gone through misunderstanding and chaos in our relationship and wondered if there was any hope for the future. Even in the depths of despair there is always the potential for a new beginning.

At times like these we reach out to our Higher Power, to our trusted friends, or to our partner for comfort and understanding. No one may have answers, and yet, when we let others share our pain, our despair and hopelessness diminish. New possibilities emerge, like a rainbow after a thunderstorm. Communication in our relationship restores us and regenerates our lives. We can pick up the pieces of what is good and create a new part in the mosaic of our lives.

Recall a time when you received
comfort from your partner
and explain how that helped you.

. . . balancing our love
for each other . . .

Someone can possess us only if we stop loving ourselves. Many popular love songs tell us that to love another we must turn ourselves over to that person completely. If we do this, of course, that person will possess us and have the power to consume our personality. But our learning about love does not stop with pop music.

True love for anyone includes loving ourselves. In the past we might have lost ourselves by assuming that the one we loved could make us feel whole or held the key to all happiness. Now by balancing love for each other with love for ourselves we can give our love joyfully and fully. We maintain this balance by nurturing our individual qualities and supporting each other. Perhaps music gives us pleasure. If we are renewed by the wilderness, we take time to be there. If reading restores us, we make time for that. As we nurture our individual gifts, we give ourselves love and also enhance our relationship.

Name a nurturing gift
you can give yourself.

. . . they are spiritual moments.

Awesome and wonderful experiences cut through our cool, doubting, or numbed exterior. They surprise us, leave us standing breathless. We are lucky when we have these experiences; they are spiritual moments. When was the last time a beautiful melody stirred us? When did we last stop to look in each other's eyes and smile in recognition? When did we last notice the intricate beauty of a lily or the graceful reach of a ball player making a catch?

We cannot force inspiring things to happen, but we can wake up to them. Awesome things are a part of everyday life. We need only to stop being numb and become alert to what is around us. We can be more aware of our senses, more curious, more open to the mysterious, more sensitive, more grateful and respectful of our experience. The spirit of life stirs in our midst.

Name something
you feel wonder at
or that stirred you recently.

The most important move is to begin.

We begin weaving by stringing vertical threads on a loom to form the foundation of a new cloth. Then horizontal threads are interlaced back and forth, and we create a fabric. As the cloth begins to form, new possibilities open before us. After we weave in the first color we can then envision other colors that will work with it. The most important move is to begin.

Sometimes new possibilities occur to us only through action. If we take the risk of the first step and keep our eyes open, we will see the next step. Too much planning, too much carefulness and analysis, may block all action.

With our partner we might sometimes feel stuck in a pattern. We may even feel hopeless. Rather than thinking excessively, we could take action, do one thing that we know people in good relationships do. We might be able to take the risk of that first step with the help of our Higher Power. When we take one hopeful step at a time, each step produces information that leads to the next.

Name one interesting thing you can do today. You need not justify it or understand where it will lead. Just try it.

. . . open up to hope
and new possibilities . . .

Some mornings we may awaken filled with thoughts of what is wrong in our lives. Perhaps we obsess about our failures or the limits of our relationships. If we let ourselves sink into self-loathing, we build a wall that separates us from those things that nurture us and give us joy.

When we awaken to the living and growing world, our spirits lift and open up to hope and new possibilities. Walking along an old sidewalk or across an abandoned parking lot, we see cracks in the concrete or asphalt and new green growth pushing through. Where there is enough soil to hold a seed, there is the possibility of a tree someday. The universe seizes opportunities for renewal that slip through the slightest opening. There is always hope for renewal in our relationships when we are willing to plant the seeds and feed them so they can grow.

Name an experience that has shown you
the seeds for new growth.

. . . we do not plot our path alone.

What we call achievement is often more gift than accomplishment. For example, healing from an illness comes partly by the grace of God. It is not forged by our will or even by trying hard. We do all that we can to get well; then we get ready to accept healing when it comes. Likewise, we might try hard to find a life partner and develop a nourishing relationship, yet we cannot accomplish this simply by setting our mind to the task. Of course we need to do what we can and we may exert great effort, but progress always takes us in directions we never fully control. Our hungry ego relishes the chance to say "I worked hard and I deserve everything I've got." But if we never stop to say "Thanks, this is wonderful" when we receive a gift, we miss an opportunity to feel lucky and grateful.

The effort to grow and learn life's lessons might lead our ego to feel we deserve total credit for our successes. But our reward is not always the one we hoped for. Sometimes we first think we get failure when we actually get inner strength and understanding, which reminds us that we do not plot our path alone.

Name gifts in your life that you worked for but still did not create.

. . . a partner who provided a place to climb.

Once when climbing rocks with friends, a woman reached a place she decided was impossible to move beyond. She wanted to retreat, but her belayer encouraged her to try again. She felt angry and scared, and she was stuck. She fought with the rock, but it was clear that the rock was never going to change. Wanting the rock to be different, to grow new footholds or handholds, was futile. After she vented her feelings, she realized there were only two ways out of her predicament. One way was to quit, and the other was to try again, perhaps with a different mind-set than she had before. Staying with her task in spite of her fear, she began to think of the rock as her friend, as a partner who provided a place to climb. She realized that she did not have to make her friend, the rock, change in order to continue climbing. Her thoughts were more focused, and she was able to make her way up the rock.

Sometimes our partner feels like an immovable rock. It is difficult to stop trying to change our partner and focus on ourselves. When we do, we discover a new direction in our relationship, a new view of our partner, and empowerment for ourselves.

Name one way your partner is strong,
like a rock.

Each candle of hope we light . . .

At times we may feel overwhelmed or depressed by the agony and the injustice in our world. But we can make a difference. Our attitudes, our values, and our actions influence our relationships. Each candle of hope we light casts hope beyond our own circle.

When we read or hear about the despair or abuse inflicted on someone somewhere, we may take on that despair and feel hopeless about everything. That attitude will surely keep us down and become part of the darkness. But if we live by our values and express our caring, we find our relationships casting new light. The love and care we share with those close to us, and with the strangers we meet on our path, spread outward to an ever-widening community of people. Each effort we make to share our brighter, caring side makes the world a better place. It makes us feel more hopeful and our connections more positive.

*Choose one small thing
you can do today to increase hope and
love around you.*

. . . push ourselves into a new perspective.

Often we become so immersed in the busy-ness of our lives that we cannot see beyond the Big Self. Immersion in our own troubles blocks healthy communication with our partner. Maybe this happens when we feel overwhelmed. At times like these we need to push ourselves into a new perspective.

Shifting our focus to helping others, or to comforting someone else, provides a fresh viewpoint on our own situation. This may be a good time to go to the closet to pull out clothing we no longer use and donate it to needy people, or to volunteer at a shelter for the homeless or abused. Or we might think of other ways to reach out to someone in need. Beyond our partnership with each other we are partners in life with the whole human community. Reaching out to help those in need transforms us and restores us to a healthy balance.

Do one thing today that will help someone else.

. . . new lives we would like to seek . . .

We dream together about adventures we would like to pursue, new lives we would like to seek, and opportunities we would like to explore. We wonder what we would have to give up to choose another path. Maybe the risks seem too big and frightening to put our dreams into action. One couple longed to take a vacation in the mountains but never broke free to try it. Another couple talked for years about moving to Alaska to start a new life, but fear always held them back.

Life is a risk, and risk brings fear. Perhaps those who avoid all risk maintain their safety, but they do not truly diminish their fear. They do not fully live. They miss the excitement of trying and the success of going forward in spite of their fear. They miss the learning that comes from mistakes and the joy of being fully alive.

Name a risk that you can take
to fulfill a dream.

. . . the ground from which we grow.

Gardening is a wonderful metaphor for life. We dig in the dirt, unearth remnants of last year's plants, adding fertilizer and compost to enrich the soil. Perhaps we find an old rusty wheel from a child's toy or uncover a tool we had lost. Similarly, we dig through our lives, uncovering old wounds, memories, and the treasures of past connections. Our past provides the ground from which we grow. We must claim it if we are to grow. Both the pain and happiness fertilize new directions for growth. The rich, black soil that nourishes this year's plants is the decomposed matter of many generations of plant life. Without the past, the present would be barren.

Now we stop to notice our partner's appearance and make a loving comment, or we express a wish for the future. Today's interactions are seeds we throw into our soil that will flower and bear fruit for us tomorrow.

Name something in your history that provides fertile ground for you today.

. . . save something to give at home . . .

"I gave at the office" is a well-known reply to solicitors for charity, but unfortunately we sometimes come home to our partner with that same attitude. We go off to work in the morning, give our best spirit and energy to our work, then come home too exhausted to give much to our personal lives. Sometimes it seems as if we come home not to be with our partner or our family, but to recover so we can go back to work. In that mind-set we bring home only our needs, our expectations, and our paychecks, not our talents, our energy, or our readiness to participate in family relationships.

At work we give our best, but in private, for ourselves and our mates, we serve only leftovers. This pattern leaves us hungry and looking to our mate for care and sustenance. If we do not save something so we can also give at home, we may feel like well-meaning, hardworking souls who just innocently ended up with an unfulfilling relationship.

Name three places where you give your energy and spirit. Do you save some to give at home?

The best things in life
are worth the work.

Some people say that if they have to work on
their relationship it must be already coming to an
end. They believe that a relationship should be
easy and fun. If it requires work or feels difficult
they take this as a sure sign that it is over.

We would do better to think of relationship work
the same way we think of the effort needed to keep
up our homes or our cars. If someone said a house
that needs work is not worth saving, we would
immediately see the foolishness in such an idea.
Everything we love requires some work and maintenance. Naturally we long for the return of the
innocence and joy that might have existed fleeting-
ly in our parents' arms or in the romantic beginning of our relationship, when all came easily.
Those times will return, but we can never com-
mand them or hold on to them permanently.
Sometimes life is hard. Some of the best things in
life are worth the work they demand.

Talk with your partner to see
what kind of maintenance your relationship
might need.

Awareness gives us the power . . .

The patterns of our lives bring comfort and security. Some of them are eternal. Some may also bring boredom, dismay, and grief. As a new day dawns we start out refreshed, and by day's end we are tired again. When we celebrate a holiday, it is not just a day off work, it is a return to a familiar symbol in our lives. Within each pattern are the seeds of renewal.

Some patterns sadden us, such as when we have the same relationship problems today as last year or the same as in our last relationship, or when we suddenly hear in our voice the echo of our overcritical mother or father, or when we lose control and reenact behavior we vowed we would never repeat. But with awareness comes renewal, even out of discouragement. At the moment we say "There I go again!" we rise above the pattern, because we see it. Awareness gives us the power to step out of a frustrating pattern into renewal.

Name one pattern in your life
you are aware of today.

We can never be an effective fixer.

Relationships with our partner's relatives can be complicated and difficult. We can get caught up in the tensions of their old family conflicts by fighting our mate's battles, by unwittingly getting drawn into the tension between them, or by expecting them to fulfill our unmet needs. If we play the go-between in old family issues, we can become a new target in old battles. Perplexed as we may be about our partner's family relationships, we can never be an effective fixer. The love between ourselves and our in-laws grows when we accept our powerlessness over their relationships.

We can keep our own honesty in relationships. We can be part of the give-and-take of extended family by giving up all attempts to be anyone's savior, teacher, or rescuer, and by leaving the unfinished issues from our own family at home.

Talk with your partner
about one of the ways you
get drawn into old family business.

Our actions touch each other.

For a tree to grow it needs the help of the sun and the rain and the soil. When it dies, it enriches the soil that it joins with and opens the soil to the sun and rain for other new growth. Even losing a branch in a storm affects all other living things that share its space. We humans are also part of a natural network. When something troubling or joyful happens to one person, it makes a difference to others. On some level they also feel it, even if they cannot name it. If another person suffers a loss or is diminished in any way, it makes a difference in our own lives.

As one part of a couple, our actions touch each other profoundly whether we intend them to or not. We need these connections. Like the roots and branches on a tree, we thrive upon our connection to the whole.

Name the human connections that feel most important to you.

When we admit
the truth to ourselves . . .

Anyone who grew up in a family where there was abuse was deeply affected by it. Maybe we did not suffer directly from physical, verbal, or sexual abuse. Perhaps we watched a parent become lost in self-abuse through alcohol, work, or food. All families have some trouble. Thomas Fuller said, "One who has no fools, knaves, nor beggars in one's family was begat by a flash of lighting." Real life is made of real-life problems and imperfections.

Sometimes we want to varnish the truth to shield our pain. Being abused, growing up with an alcoholic parent, or worrying about a brother in trouble may instill in us feelings of unworthiness and shame. These are by-products, feelings left over in the aftermath of abuse and addiction. They do not represent our true value as human beings. When we admit the truth to ourselves and remove the varnish from our experience, we can grow out of our shame.

Name some problem in your family that
you or others have tried to hide.

JOINT PURPOSE

Joint purposes guide our actions.

We can have purpose and direction for our relationship, just as a team, a company, or a school has purposes. Individually, we may be dedicated to a career, a worthy cause, and caring for our children. As a couple, our joint purposes may be less obvious, but they do guide our actions and choices. Are we dedicated to enjoying life together, raising healthy children, and making a contribution to the good of all people? Or are we dedicated to amassing a large financial estate, getting sexual satisfaction, and looking good to others?

We can get swept into pursuing unworthy goals if we passively follow shiny empty images around us. But by intentionally selecting our purposes and staying true to them, we connect with our Higher Power. Working for goals that are bigger than ourselves and our need for gratification will carry us beyond our own ego. It boosts morale in our relationship and helps us wisely choose our actions.

Name some team goals
of your relationship.

. . . made of many threads.

On one day what we think is a dominating truth about our relationship may seem like a minor reality another day. At one time we think "He never listens to me," or "She and I are so different it's a wonder that we ever got together." Another day, under other circumstances, our frustrations feel minor. Then we believe the negative aspects of the relationship are not important because our connection feels so rewarding in other ways.

A strong rope is made of many threads. Looking at one point on the rope, we can focus on the detail of a single thread. But when we look only at a single thread we cannot see the big picture. Likewise, today's thoughts and feelings about our relationship, as important as they are, will change as our perspective changes. Today, focusing on one feeling, we may reach a conclusion about our relationship, a conclusion that may change later. As we grow together, the detail of today blends with the complex bundle of threads that are each important in the big picture.

Say what the details feel like today in your relationship; then say what you think the big picture looks like.

*. . . keep returning to
and renewing our love.*

We all change in time. We become different people than we once were and force our relationships to shift. Circumstances around us also change and force us to face unexpected challenges. Successful relationships have many kinds of support to help maintain them through time. Romance alone is never enough. Need and dependency are not enough. Kids are not enough. A formal promise given in a marriage ceremony and supported legally can sustain our relationship, but we know that is not enough either.

We all need to keep returning to and renewing our love, especially during challenging times. We need mutual friends who know and love us both and with whom we can socialize. Similar values help. Shared pleasures or interests help. A common goal or purpose helps. Joint membership in a club, synagogue, church, or community group helps. The support of extended family helps. Working together and playing together help. Besides romance, these practical and realistic factors all help relationships succeed over the long haul.

Talk with your mate about the things that help sustain your relationship over time.

Commitment liberates us.

When the topic of commitment comes up, some of us squirm. We chafe under the idea because we think of commitment as a restraint, like a harness on a horse. Who would want to enter a commitment that feels like a harness? Some submit to escape their insecurity and avoid loneliness. But we know that image of commitment is not healthy.

Commitment does put limits on us. But we choose commitment because it liberates us more than it confines us. Commitment is a doorway to the realm of a stronger, freer life. So we commit to walk through the doorway by pledging to be honest with each other, to be faithful, and to support each other during times when we are weak or troubled. We promise to take care of ourselves so we can be a strong partner. This type of commitment liberates us by allowing us to have more choices, by making life easier, and by freeing us to go out to meet our challenges and enjoy the lighter moments more fully.

*Name your commitments
to each other.*

*. . . more willing to give
our energy.*

After hard times, some people become more awake than before—more deeply appreciative of a true love, more easily moved by the simple pleasure of a beautiful song, more able to enjoy a good talk with a friend. When we have hurt someone we love, or when we have been hurt by our mate, we might become more committed to tending and caring for our partnership. Whether the hurts are old or new, after we know the pain of relationship difficulty we are more willing to give our energy to avoid it.

Conscious commitment to a good life becomes a choice we eagerly make because it feels much better than helplessness, making no choice, and enduring emotional pain. Choosing to do something, even when it is difficult, energizes us for the hard work of partnership. So we consciously say what is hard to say, break through barriers of resistance to honesty, and bring our ideas to our partnership. Yes, it is difficult to do sometimes, but we choose this difficulty of awareness over the difficulty of blindness.

*Name something you do consciously to
enrich your partnership.*

The feeling of belonging is a gift.

The feeling of belonging—knowing that we have a place—is one of the most important gifts that two partners can give to each other. When we agree to commit ourselves to a partnership, we give each other the key to our daily lives. We allow our mate to be there with us in a way we would not let others. That means that we can expect to have a place that does not have to be renegotiated every day. This feeling of belonging is a gift, but it must be received. In essence, we say to our partner, "I take my place here in your life because we have our relationship. I will relax. I don't stand at the door and knock. We have already told each other that we are included in each other's lives."

This sense of belonging stands in sharp contrast to those feelings of isolation and alienation that we can feel in so many ways. It does not mean that one partner owns the other or that no boundary or separateness exists. But the joy of connection frees people in relationships to fulfill themselves and carry on their lives while in the close comfort of one they love.

Tell your partner how you know you have a place in her or his life.

INDEX

143

More great ideas from Hazelden...

True Selves
Twelve Step Recovery from Codependency
   by Roseann Lloyd and Merle Fossum
   A life-affirming guide to recovery, with thought-provoking photographs. For all adults who have been lost in their relationships or who have never learned to be true to themselves, *True Selves* is a mixture of tested ideas, nurturing poetry, personal stories, and reassurance. A refreshing look at how you define the boundaries between self and others, and the importance of self-love and self-care. 129 pp.

Order No. 5140

Loving Me, Loving You
Balancing Love and Power in a Codependent World
   by Brenda Schaeffer
   From the popular author of *Is It Love or Is It Addiction?* comes practical advice on how to leave or avoid love addiction. Using charts, lists, and exercises, this book helps you understand what you can do to reach a healthy balance of love and power in your relationship. A new look at the spiritual and emotional energy available to you through personal transformation. 232 pp.

Order No. 5154

For price and order information, or a free catalog, please call our Telephone Representatives.

HAZELDEN EDUCATIONAL MATERIALS
   Pleasant Valley Road • P.O. Box 176
   Center City, MN 55012-0176
   1-800-328-9000 (toll-free U.S., Canada, Virgin Islands)
   1-612-257-4010 (outside the U.S. & Canada)
   1-612-257-1331 (FAX)

HAZELDEN EUROPE • Cork, Ireland
   (Int'l code) + 353-21-314318